If you haven't yet discovered your pl[...]  [...]st
looking for more clarity, this book is [...]
    —**DAVE FERGUSON,** lead vi[...]
    NewThing; author, *Hero Make*[...]

If you want to see big things happen in your life and work, *Find Your Place*
is your go-to companion.
    —**RANDY FRAZEE,** pastor; author *The Connecting Church 2.0*

Find Your Place has challenged me to lean into who God has called me to
love and how I can leverage my unique wiring to put love into action.
    —**TONY MORGAN,** founder and lead strategist, The Unstuck Group

People serious about following Jesus and finding their place in Jesus' mission to restore all things need to read this book.
    —**ALAN HIRSCH,** founder, 100 Movements,
    Forge, and 5Q collective; author

Rob and Brian help you discover where you are now, discover where you
need to be, and provide ways to discover the path to get there.
    —**NEIL COLE,** apostolic catalyst of organic church movements;
    author, *Organic Church*

Invite Rob and Brian, through this book, to be your guides in discovering
and embracing God's calling on your life.
    —**DANIEL IM,** author, *No Silver Bullets*

If you struggle with knowing what you should do with your life, this book
is for you.
    —**DR. RICHARD L. PRATT JR.,** president,
    Third Millennium Ministries

The best people to write a book on personal calling are ones who have
relentlessly optimized their own. *Find Your Place* provides a clear road-
map for others to follow.
    —**STEVE GLADEN,** pastor of small groups,
    Saddleback Church

I highly recommend that every church purchase several copies of this book and take all of their leaders and potential leaders through it. It will make a difference!

—**CHRIS SURRATT,** author, *Small Groups for the Rest of Us*

This is not theory, it is practice. This book is a must read for anyone who is serious about making disciples and developing leaders.

—**DAN SOUTHERLAND,** author, *Transitions*

Brian and Rob have done some amazing work. Do yourself a favor and learn from their decades of ministry.

—**BEN REED,** adult ministries pastor, MISSION Community Church

This book is a game changer. Read it and then give this practical, clear, and life-changing book to every Christian you know. They will "rise up and call you blessed."

—**STEVE BROWN,** founder, Key Life Network;
author; seminary professor

Daily I talk with people about their calling. I will recommend *Find Your Place* to people who are looking to reach their full potential for the mission of Jesus.

—**JANET MCMAHON,** community life pastor,
Restore Community Church

Wow, where has this book been? It could radically change Christianity in America from attendance driven to fulfillment living for each individual made in the image of God.

—**EDDIE MOSLEY,** adult groups minister, Brentwood Baptist Church

Find Your Place is exactly what every church member needs. Once you apply these truths, your life, your church, and your community will never be the same.

—**ALLEN WHITE,** author, *Exponential Groups:
Unleashing Your Church's Potential*

Find Your Place has changed my life, my family's lives, and my business. Read it only if you are truly interested in being activated into His mission for your life.

—**ANDY TRAUB,** president, Traub and Associates Consulting

FIND YOUR PLACE

FIND YOUR PLACE

LOCATING YOUR CALLING THROUGH
YOUR GIFTS, PASSIONS, AND STORY

ROB WEGNER AND BRIAN PHIPPS

ZONDERVAN®

MADE FOR MORE
RESOURCES

ZONDERVAN REFLECTIVE

Find Your Place
Copyright © 2019 by Rob Wegner and Brian Phipps

ISBN 978-0-310-10719-4 (audio)

Requests for information should be addressed to:
Zondervan, *3900 Sparks Dr. SE, Grand Rapids, Michigan 49546*

Library of Congress Cataloging-in-Publication Data

Names: Wegner, Rob, 1970- author. | Phipps, Brian, 1967- author.
Title: Find your place : locating your calling through your gifts, passions, and story /
    Rob Wegner and Brian Phipps.
Description: Grand Rapids, Michigan : Zondervan, [2019] | Includes bibliographical references. |
Identifiers: LCCN 2019005800 (print) | LCCN 2019014701 (ebook) | ISBN 9780310100133 (ebook) |
    ISBN 9780310100126 (pbk.)
Subjects: LCSH: Vocation--Christianity. | Gifts, Spiritual. | Character tests.
Classification: LCC BV4740 (ebook) | LCC BV4740 .W39 2019 (print) | DDC 248.4--dc23
LC record available at https://lccn.loc.gov/2019005800

Published in association with the literary agency of Mark Sweeney & Associates, Naples, Florida 34113.

Cover design: Rick Szuecs Design
Cover art: Harryarts / Freepiks.com
Interior design: Kait Lamphere

Printed in the United States of America

22 23 24 25 26 27 28 29 30 31 32 33 /LSC/ 15 14 13 12 11 10 9 8 7 6 5 4 3 2

First of all, we dedicate this book to our kids—Hannah, Sam, and Caleb on the Phipps team, and Maddie, Whit, and Belle on the Wegner team. It is our deep desire that you know that you were born on purpose, with a purpose, for a purpose. The world needs you to find your place. We believe in you. We are for you. Jesus has a one-of-a-kind masterpiece mission designed for you. We commit our lives to serving you so you can find your place.

Second, we dedicate this book to every follower of Jesus who has accepted the challenge to identify, develop, and optimize their personal calling. You are the heroes of this book. We believe you are the future of the church. Whether you are a stay-at-home mom or dad, a city clerk, an architect, a medical doctor, a college freshman, a line worker, or a senator, your calling matters. The world also needs you to find your place. We believe in you. We are for you!

May the stories and insights in these pages help you find the way to *your* place. Do what you can do because only you can do it.

CONTENTS

FOREWORD BY TODD WILSON

We are God's masterpiece. He has created us
anew in Christ Jesus, so we can do the good
things he planned for us long ago.
—*Ephesians 2:10 NLT*

Followers of Jesus are made for more. We want the life that Jesus offers, but we fall short of taking hold of the abundant life he made possible, abundance that is found in discovering and engaging the purposes God designed for each of us. Instead of living life to the fullest measure by finding our personal callings, we trod through life, dreaming of better days. Followers of Jesus in America have been conditioned to settle for less.

In Ephesians 2:10, Paul tells us that followers of Jesus are saved for far more than a destination. They are saved to play a part in the grand restoration of God's kingdom on earth.

Christians are recreated in Jesus for a purpose and with inherent significance. These recreated individuals have a hunger to play the part Jesus planned for them, but many if not most will not realize that calling.

The term calling refers to the spiritual summons from God to find our identity in Jesus and to be disciples who make disciples wherever we find ourselves. This common or general calling unites us on a common mission with all other Christians throughout time.

In contrast, our unique calling distinguishes us from all other Christians and equips us to do the "good things" Jesus planned for each of us to do. Our unique calling finds its significance in the context of our common or general calling to make disciples. God equips each of us with a personal calling to more effectively play our part in making disciples wherever we go in corners of society.

According to Ephesians 2, every follower of Jesus receives this sacred summons. In America, however, this term has been used almost exclusively for pastors, missionaries, or other church leaders in vocational ministry. This tragedy has not simply squelched the potential impact of the church in America, it has put it in a chokehold.

In recent years, a growing number of church leaders are taking a step back and putting their sights on a better path forward. There is a growing sense that something is wrong with our system of volunteerism. Most churches have embraced a "we can do it, you can help" posture that is vital to running the programs of the church. Unfortunately, this approach tends not to mobilize people within their unique calling.

What we need is a "you can do it, we can help" posture that seeks to equip and mobilize God's people to accomplish God's purposes wherever that leads them. Imagine the impact of a movement of Jesus followers mobilized into all corners of society within the context of their unique callings!

It is now time for followers of Jesus to take the next step. It is time for every follower to pursue, locate, and make the highest possible impact through their personal calling. Sometimes that calling is within the walls of a local church ministry. More and more, however, the aperture of calling potential is being opened up to include every nook and cranny of the world.

Followers of Jesus are being called to engage the fight against loneliness, poverty, and other forms of injustice. Followers of Jesus are influencing enterprise and the marketplace to value their people instead of using them. Jesus is leading more and more of his people into mission where they live, work, study, and play. I believe Jesus has called each of his followers in a way that would meet every need in every community if only they had a way to locate that calling.

If you are sensing God's summons, if you are hearing Jesus calling you to become more, then this book is for you. *Find Your Place* provides a helpful language and a clear and proven pathway for you to locate and take a next step in your calling. *Find Your Place* is filled with stories of people, just like you, who have moved from simply volunteering in a church to joining Jesus in his mission, extending the influence of their churches into their communities and around the world.

Rob Wegner and Brian Phipps have made the pursuit of personal calling practical and attainable. They had *you* in mind the whole time they were writing this book. Rob and Brian are proven practitioners who have mobilized hundreds and even thousands of people to locate their callings and make the kind of impact for which they were recreated.

I wish this book had been available while I wrestled with my calling.

I was a nuclear engineer with a successful and satisfying career. In many ways, I was living the American dream. But my success fueled a discontent that left me longing for significance. I spent two full years before reluctantly taking a next step, and then another decade journeying to find my place.

My passion for starting healthy new churches continues to increase, and I now spend most of my energy engaged in a wide range of leading-edge and pioneering initiatives aimed at helping catalyze movements of healthy, reproducing churches. Before discovering my calling, I never could have imagined doing what I'm doing now. Discovering our calling opens new and exciting doors into the future.

I cannot imagine what life would be like had Jesus not

led me to locate my calling. I cringe at the thought of potentially spending a lifetime pursuing success while missing out on the life Jesus meant for me.

You're probably reading this book because you want to be a good steward of the life Jesus intends for you to take hold of. Rob and Brian's book will help you discover and engage your calling. Lean into it. Work through their exercises. Prayerfully anticipate what God will reveal to you as you journey through this gem of a resource.

The Spirit of God—the same Spirit who hovered over the darkness at creation, the same Spirit who raised Jesus from the dead, the same Spirit who changed your life—is still hovering over the recreation that is you, waiting to show you the gifts he has deposited in you, waiting to help you see the passions that he has instilled in you, waiting to show you the next step in your story.

As the Spirit's power enters the depths of your soul, fusing your daily life with your eternal purpose, an awakening will stir within you that will cause you never to settle for less again.

Join me in the journey that is living on mission with Jesus through your calling. Enjoy this book and enjoy the ride.

ACKNOWLEDGMENTS

We are grateful to so many for their meaningful contributions to *Find Your Place*. We are grateful for Bruce Bugby and Network Ministries for their foundational work in raising the awareness of personal calling in the church. We are grateful for Rick Warren and Saddleback Church's Class 301 (S.H.A.P.E.), which helped us see how personal calling is a critical part of making disciples. Both of these resources shaped how we led in our ministry settings.

We are grateful for the thousands of people who have been the "beneficiaries" of our disciple-making efforts over the years. Our investment in each other has resulted in this book, which will impact not simply the readers of this book but also the thousands of people in their circles as they serve through their personal callings. Thank you for growing with us!

We are grateful for Michelle Wicker, Kelly Maxwell, and Amy Dmyterko, who helped us shape the GPS assessment and process from which this book evolved. We are grateful for Shelly Arnold, Breanna Wiebe, and Joe Klassen (the rest of the Next Steps team!) for helping us develop the personal callings of hundreds of people at Westside Family Church. Most of the stories in this book, and much of the insights shared in it, emerged from the experience of making disciples with this team. We are grateful for Kelly Maxwell, who helped us early on with editing the initial manuscript.

We are grateful for our families too. They have put up with us as we bounced our ideas of developing personal calling off of them. They were the guinea pigs, taking the early, middle, and late versions of the online GPS assessment. They were patient with us as we spent time away writing. We are grateful!

INTRODUCTION

Three years ago, my family and I set out on a journey. (Cue high-pitched singing: "Follow the yellow brick road!")

After twenty years of living in South Bend, Indiana, we left what was safe and predictable, launching out to relocate in Kansas. Some saw it as a hairbrained adventure. Our two oldest daughters, Maddie and Whitney, were transitioning into high school, and it was not a good time to uproot them. They led a pitchfork uprising over the move! On top of that, my wife, Michelle, is a freelance writer, and she had just hustled her way into writing positions for three successful regional magazines. This had not been easy, and it was not something she was ready to walk away from. Our youngest, Belle, was the only one in the family ready to make the trip!

I had no reason to leave either. I was on staff at one of the most influential churches in America, surrounded by people we loved and had shared our lives with for a long time. Many in the congregation likely assumed that in a few years, I would be the lead pastor. If vocational ministry were simply a career path to be managed, staying in my pastoral role would have been a no-brainer.

Yet here we were, with our house in South Bend unsold, on the yellow brick road (otherwise known as I-72), headed west to begin a new life in Kansas City. Michelle was driving our yellow jeep, accompanied by our two dogs, Mori and Ellie. I was stuffed in the minivan with the rest of our gang, a couple miles ahead of Michelle. We had never made this drive before and didn't know the way, but we had our map app open on our phones and were following the directions and prompts as the GPS tracked our progress and guided us to our new home.

In my rearview mirror, I noticed a big, black SUV approaching at high speed. As the driver flew by me, I saw he was looking down at his lap. He was tussling with an old-school paper map, trying to read it while driving! The map was draped over his steering wheel and pushed up onto the windshield.

I was stunned.

What in the world? Who pays fifty thousand dollars for a vehicle, and another several hundred for a smartphone with GPS, and then risks his life (and ours) by using a paper map? My first thought was, "Get out of the Stone Age, dude."

Not more than two minutes later, my phone rang. It was Michelle. I could hear her breathing heavy, her voice filled with fear.

"Rob, I almost just died. I was cut off by this guy who came swerving over into my lane, and I had to slam on the brakes. We spun around, and I ended up in the ditch. I don't think he even saw me. He was wrestling a huge map and didn't have his eyes on the road."

Map-man had almost killed my wife.

To say I was furious would be an understatement. So I headed after Map-man in hot pursuit. Our minivan hit speeds it had never seen before. Unfortunately, Map-man's vehicle was faster—and more important, my road rage abated and clear thinking prevailed. At the next exit, I turned around to check on Michelle. We found her several miles back, scared but okay. After some hugs and a few deep breaths, we were back on the road, grateful for the gift of life—and thankful for our GPS.

We knew God had a clear direction for us. We weren't turning back.

Now, I don't know Map-man. I'm not sure why he was in such a hurry. And I have no idea why he was using a paper map on the interstate. But here's a general observation. Men are notorious for not wanting to ask for directions. If a guy is lost, to ask for directions or let the GPS tell him where to go means admitting defeat. Most guys I know can recall a time when they tried to find their way, only to end up in the middle of nowhere, as in *Deliverance* or *10 Cloverfield Lane*, all because they wouldn't ask for directions.

The truth, if we're humble enough to admit it, is that we need help. We need guidance to get us where we are supposed to be, especially when we're in foreign territory, heading in a new direction.

THE WHAT

Getting directions is easier than it's ever been. With the advent of GPS (Global Positioning System) and computerized mapping software, navigation has been revolutionized. These products have made it possible for anyone—even the most prone to wander—to accurately find their way to their destination.

The Global Positioning System relies on twenty-four satellites orbiting our planet, which send time-stamped information to your phone or navigation system. Your device picks up those signals and then instantaneously calculates how long it takes for the signals to arrive. If your GPS unit receives four signals, it can locate you by working out your precise distance from each of the satellites, triangulating your exact position on the planet.

The Global Positioning System was developed by an agency known as DARPA (Defense Advanced Research Projects Agency). DARPA runs super-advanced research for our military. Although DARPA creates future-tense, covert technology designed for folks like Jason Bourne or James Bond, eventually that technology ends up in everyone's hands. If you use the internet, a microwave, a computer, or even duct tape—yes, duct tape!—you can thank DARPA. At one point, these amazing inventions were available to only a select few. Now they're everywhere.

And that's why you carry a GPS device wherever you go.

I know what you're thinking. That's an interesting history lesson, but why should I care about the how and why of GPS?

Well, we're glad you asked. We think GPS is an incredibly helpful tool for locating where you are and finding your destination. But this book isn't a user manual for orienteering or geocaching. We aren't interested in helping you find your way across town or giving you advice for your next road trip. We want to talk about you. Your gifts, your passions, and your story.

Wouldn't it be great if there were GPS for the soul?

We've all had times in life when we've felt lost. Maybe you feel that way right now. We're continually haunted by the ancient, existential questions that people of every culture and generation ask.

- Why am I here?
- What is my purpose?
- What is my unique contribution to the planet?
- What is my calling?

What if there were a spiritual technology that could help you answer those questions and intuit your God-given calling? What if this "soul tech" could help you perceive your own time-stamped spiritual signals, then triangulate your position and give you real-time direction to show you where you need to go next? What if this were available to everyone, not just the spiritual elite?

We've written this book, *Find Your Place*, because this spiritual technology exists. And it's not a covert technology. It's for all of us. It's available to you today. You can fumble around with a crumbled paper map of mere human guesswork, hoping that someday you will find out where you are and where you are heading. But if you take the crumbled-map approach to living—like Map-man on the interstate—you run the risk of not only wasting your life but robbing others of theirs as well.

There's a better way. We want to invite you to learn about the God-designed soul technology of GPS:

- Gifts
- Passions
- Story

We all need direction to get where we are supposed to be. If you are guessing your way through life, chances are you aren't going anywhere. Sure, it can seem exciting for a while, but eventually you end up lost and confused, frustrated that your life hasn't turned out the way you thought it would.

So how do you find your place? How do you locate your calling? Your gifts, passions, and story can get you there.

Your gifts, passions, and story—each of these are sending you a different signal. And when those signals are triangulated by the Spirit of God through a community of trusted traveling companions, they will tell you where you are right now and where you need to be.

Remember our trip down the yellow brick road to Kansas? As we drove on the highway, we were following the directions of a smartphone, relying on technical GPS to guide us. But even more important, we were following a spiritual GPS. Uprooting from the life we had known for more than two decades was costly and difficult. But we had a clear sense that God wanted us in Kansas City. We looked at our gifts. We considered our passions. We reflected on our story. And today, four years into our new adventure, we are saying to ourselves, "We are exactly where we are supposed to be!"

About a year after our move, as we were talking and praying together before bed, our youngest daughter prayed, "Jesus, thank you for moving us to Kansas City. We've never been closer to you or each other." Following our spiritual GPS has led us to experience greater peace, meaning, and confidence in our lives, and that is priceless.

Throughout this book, we (Rob and Brian) want to help you learn how to turn up the reception level of these three signals—your gifts, passions, and story—so you can triangulate them into a clear sense of direction, leading you closer to your personal calling.

What could matter more?

This book is a partnership between two friends. We are writing this book together, and while most of the book will have a single, united voice, at times we'll share personal stories and examples from our lives. So you'll find us slipping in and out of the driver's seat during the journey. Don't worry, we'll try to make sure you know who's at the wheel. Most of the time, we'll note this by placing one of our names in parentheses when we switch drivers.

THE WHY

I (Brian) also know the value of GPS technology. I've purchased a GPS unit for myself, for my wife, and for each of my driving children. And like Rob, I know the value of utilizing soul GPS. I was twenty-five years old, attending seminary in preparation for pastoral ministry, when I took my first spiritual gift assessment. At the time, I had a deep sense that I was called to ministry, but to be honest, I had no real understanding of what that meant. All I knew was that I was supposed to go to seminary and someday become a preacher.

In 1 Corinthians 12:1, the apostle Paul writes about spiritual gifts, saying, "Now about the gifts of the Spirit, brothers and sisters, I do not want you to be uninformed." I was a lifetime churchgoer and a second-year seminary student, but I found I was uninformed—not only about my own spiritual gifts but about how to help others discover and use their gifts. I was clueless!

You might assume that the seminary I was attending provided the gifts assessment to help in my training. But sadly, it wasn't the seminary asking me to take my first gifts assessment. Jon Taylor, the pastor of the small church where I was serving as the youth director, forced me to take it. Initially, I was irritated. In my pride and arrogance, I wondered why I, a seminary student, would need help figuring out my calling. I had already discerned what I was going to do with my life. I was in seminary to be a pastor. Certainly, I of all people did not need to take the test!

But I didn't get a choice. So I took the dumb test.

The results of the assessment made me even more upset. They indicated that my strongest gift was teaching, and nothing else showed up after that. My mother was a middle school teacher, and I knew that was the *last* thing I wanted to be. At that point, I was ready to quit, but God had a different plan.

Pastor Jon took the results and did something brilliant. He invited me to join him in developing a curriculum to train our elders. I realized I wasn't bothered by this request, and in fact the invitation was more alluring to me than a great big steak and a baked potato. I was carrying a heavy load of classes, taking sixteen hours at the master's degree level, while also working part-time, but I found that I had an interest in and a passion for this task. I dove right into the assignment. And once I got started, I couldn't quit. It consumed me. Within a few weeks, I had written an entire survey of the Bible, with a focus on covenant theology.

Before I finish my story, I want you to catch something here. That "dumb" gift assessment I was forced to take somehow drilled its way into the depths of my soul. It uncorked a reservoir of passion I didn't know I had. Pastor Jon never needed to push me to complete the curriculum.

The initiative, interest, and passion to accomplish that work came from within me. My motivation was intrinsic, and I enjoyed doing it as much as anything else I had ever done! My roommates thought I was weird. Pastor Jon probably did too.

But I was hooked. Through that experience, I realized I had something more specific than a vague and intangible calling into ministry. I realized that I was called to equip disciples through teaching. That revelation has led me to spend the majority of my ministry years working in equipping roles, teaching and training other people how to follow Jesus, and I have loved every minute of it.

Merriam-Webster defines a calling as "a strong inner impulse toward a particular course of action especially when accompanied by conviction of divine influence."

I had that impulse. And I believe that impulse came from a divine place.

But it wasn't just one thing that led me and confirmed my calling. I experienced more than a simple impulse; I also experienced a tangible result that validated the impulse. As I answered the call and saw the results, God used that sense of calling to build up his people and bless others.

The elders in that church loved the curriculum I developed and taught, so much so that they invited their spouses and kids to experience it. And what those families learned motivated them to invest more of their lives into the life of our church. When I taught, I often heard people say things like, "I have been in the church for thirty years, and I have learned

more in these last two months than over that entire period"
or "You just make the Scriptures come alive." Apparently,
the bar for good teaching was very low in that church.

Seriously, though, I knew that God was up to something.
I could see how Jesus was making a difference in the lives of
others, and he was doing it through me! That was something
I had never experienced before. And to this day, I enjoy making a difference in others' lives as much as anything I have
the privilege and honor of doing.

Decades ago, a simple gift assessment helped me identify my primary gift. Using that gift to serve others tapped
into an internal passion, and discovering that passion has
shaped my life story. It has also made a difference in other
people's stories. Do you see it, how they are interconnected?

Gifts.

Passions.

Story.

We'll spend more time unpacking how these three work
together to locate our calling, but here is what I want you to
know: I believe Jesus has called every last one of his followers
into something far more powerful than a "blessed assur-
ance." Jesus, through the indwelling presence of the Holy
Spirit, *is* the divine influence Merriam-Webster references.
He has guided countless people toward the course of action
he has in mind for them. Jesus has called all of us to follow
him, and each of his followers has a divinely appointed role
to play in building up his people and influencing their story.

And the best part is that you will love playing your role.

Finding your place and your unique calling isn't something bothersome you need to add to your already busy life. Once you understand your calling, it will bring meaning to your life and drive your day-to-day decision making. Jesus wants to tap into the gifts and passions he deposited into you when you gave your life to him, and he wants to develop those gifts and hone those passions over time for his glory and your joy.

So don't worry if you are a bit of a Map-man. Even if you feel lost and confused or your life seems to be racing out of control, we can help you find your calling. You have a soul GPS. You have gifts, you have passions, and you have a story.

Are you ready to engage them?

THE HOW

Your gifts, passions, and story are the three signals that will help you triangulate your calling. There are three primary sources of those signals, each with a different way of being received and understood: an online assessment, peer feedback, and service in Jesus' kingdom. To assist you in using your GPS, we recommend the following steps.

1. *Assessment.* Take the online assessment at *www.gift passionstory.com*. The results will be invaluable as you seek to discern your calling.

2. *Peer feedback.* Share your results with your peers and ask for their feedback. Invite a friend who knows you well to take the first two sections of the online assessment as if they were you. Analyze the results of this feedback and the online assessments, taking note of the differences.

3. *Service opportunity.* Find an opportunity to serve in a role that fits what you've learned about yourself, regularly evaluating your fruitfulness and fulfillment. No one steps into their calling at full speed. You crawl, then walk, and finally run. Long-term, what you discover in this book may lead to radical change, maybe even a new career in a new location. But for now, look for a way to crawl into your calling by serving in some manner that resonates with your GPS signals. A local church or community organization is a great place to start.

Online Assessment

There are three portions to the online assessment, which will help you discover your gifts, passions, and story. The gifts portion and the passions portion include a series of multiple-choice questions, and both can be completed in less than thirty minutes. The story portion is more reflective, so the assessment guides you through a preparation process before you complete it.

When I (Brian) was growing up, we had a plaque hanging in our home that read, "Life is like a piano. What you get out of it depends on how you play it." The same is true for the assessment. Give it the time it deserves. You are looking for clues to help you understand the masterpiece God has made in you! Before you begin and as you answer the questions, spend time asking God to reveal what he wants you to see.

Peer Feedback

Your GPS results are only as reliable as the information you start with. Unfortunately, the subjective data we put into the GPS assessment can be one-dimensional; often we fail to input the most critical information. Peer feedback is essential to getting a more realistic understanding of our calling.

We recommend you ask someone who knows you well to review your GPS results with you. Ask them if they agree or disagree with any of the results and to give you reasons why, with examples. Better yet, ask them to take the assessment as if they were you, and compare the results. Then debrief the differences. Repeat this process with one or two more people, and you should have a really clear signal!

Kingdom Service

The best way to know whether you are living out Jesus' calling in your life is to serve somewhere while asking yourself two questions.

1. Is God using my service to advance his kingdom and purposes?
2. Do I experience joy, fulfillment, and a sense of purpose as I serve?[1]

If you serve where Jesus has designed you to serve, your answer to both of these questions will be a strong yes. If you see God using you to advance his purposes but you have no joy or fulfillment, you are either using your gifts in an area you aren't passionate about or serving in your area of passion but in the wrong role. If you answer no to both of these questions, it is time to ask for help from a leader in your church or a mentor in your life.

THE NOW

Consider these words from Mark Twain: "The two most important days in your life are the day you were born, and the day you find out why." There's a big difference between existing, living, and surviving and *thriving*. GPS can make the difference.

The apostle Paul said it this way: "We are God's masterpiece. He has created us anew in Christ Jesus, so we can do the good things he planned for us long ago" (Eph. 2:10 NLT).

You are a masterpiece, so you can do good works. The phrase "so we can do" from this verse, if literally translated, would be, "in order that we might walk in them." The purpose of these prepared-in-advance works is not "to work in them" but "to walk in them."[2] God has prepared a GPS path of good works that he will perform in and through you as you walk by faith. Your calling is the only pathway by which you will be able to live a fully God-empowered and God-saturated life.

It's time to start walking.

Get ready to take the assessment at *www.giftpassion story.com*. Get a pen and journal ready. Get together a team of family and friends who can join you on the GPS journey. Why don't you send a few of them an email or text message right now. Invite them to discover their calling with you.

Why make this extra effort of bringing others into the process?

Thoughts disentangle themselves through your lips and fingertips. The impact of this book will increase in direct correlation to the amount of personal journaling and community conversation you invest into it.

As you read this book, you'll be given questions to consider. Keep your journal handy, and jot down thoughts and observations immediately. As you go through this book with your GPS companions, discuss every chapter together in real time. Ask them to take the online assessment, not just for themselves but for you. You can do the same for them. It's only through this kind of 360-degree view, born of deep community feedback and deep self-reflection, that we can tune in all the signals at full strength and triangulate them, giving us clarity on our calling.

The journey into our calling begins with our gifts, passions, and story.

The discovery of that purpose begins now.

CHAPTER 1

INCOMPREHENSIBLE

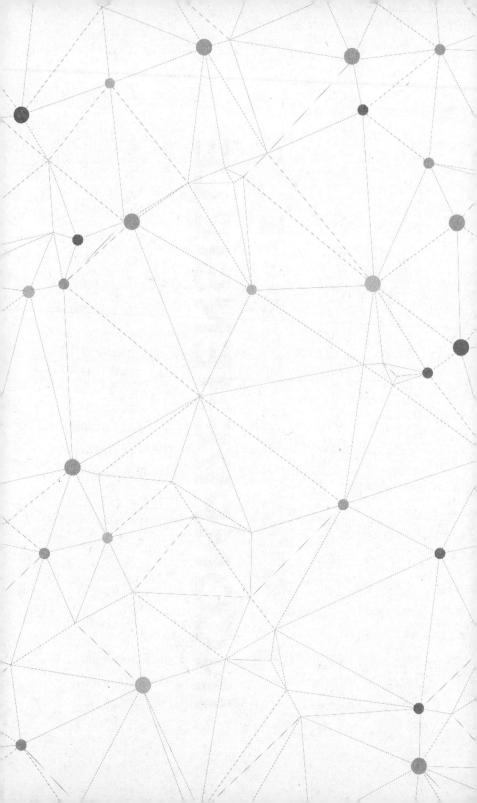

What exotic destinations are on your bucket list? For centuries, ardent travelers have compiled the ultimate destinations into a list known as the Seven Wonders of the World. Various iterations of the list exist: the Ancient Wonders, the Modern Wonders, the Natural Wonders, and so forth.

The Taj Mahal often makes the list. Sir Edwin Arnold, the English poet, describes this masterpiece with these words: "Not a piece of architecture, as other buildings are, but the proud passions of an emperor's love wrought in living stones." This ivory-white, translucent marble palace radiates like a diamond in the daytime and glows like a pearl at night. It's a shining monument that symbolizes the eternal love of the Mughal emperor Shah Jahan for his wife Mumtaz, who died during childbirth. This grand memorial was handcrafted by a small army of twenty-two thousand artisans who, over a period of twenty-two years, inlaid thousands of semiprecious stones in breathtakingly beautiful patterns. Many would say, "This is the greatest masterpiece in India."

Everyone has seen pictures of the Taj Mahal. But those who have seen it in person often say the Taj is something that can only be experienced, not described. A former US president summarized it this way: "There are two types of people in the world: those who have experienced the Taj and those who have not."

Curiously, the first time I (Rob) visited the Taj, numerous Indian tourists—total strangers—asked to have their picture taken with me and Michelle. Over a couple hours, it happened again and again! After the last photo shoot, I said to Michelle, "It's really frustrating that they keep mistaking me for Brad Pitt." Yeah, she rolled her eyes just like you did.

Honestly, the amount of attention made us both feel very uncomfortable. We're standing in front of one of the Seven Wonders of the World, the masterpiece of India, and you want a picture of a couple from Indiana? Trust me, the word Hoosiers does not appear on any of the Wonders of the World lists.

Or should it?

What if, in all our searching for the wonders of the world, we've missed the one we look at every morning in the mirror? It bears repeating: Ephesians 2:10 (NLT) reveals, "We are God's masterpiece. He has created us anew in Christ Jesus, so we can do the good things he planned for us long ago."

You are a masterpiece. You are a one-of-a-kind bearer of God's image, priceless in worth, filled with a mysterious and unique mix of gifts and passions, within an amazing story that is exclusively yours.

Saint Augustine said, "Men go abroad to wonder at the heights of mountains, at the huge waves of the sea, at the long courses of the rivers, at the vast compass of the ocean, at the circular motions of the stars, and they pass by themselves without wondering."

It's time to start wondering. Why? You're a masterpiece designed by a God who loves you more than you can imagine, whose purpose for you is unique—one in seven billion.

You're not just a speck on the time line of history. You're not an accident. You were made on purpose with a purpose for a purpose. There is a set body of good works that has your name on it. As surely as did Mother Teresa or Martin Luther King Jr., you have a calling.

You are a masterpiece.

The Taj Mahal has nothing on you.

But you're going to have to stop looking for your calling "out there" and start looking "in here." GPS is going to take you on an inner journey before you go on an outer journey. People are so obsessed with looking for the answer to their existential crisis "out there" that they fail to realize that the catalytic discoveries about one's calling start "in here."

You are a masterpiece, worthy of research and reflection. You need to get to know that masterpiece much better.

John Calvin, the most influential theologian of the Reformation era, argued that one could not truly know God without knowing oneself and that one couldn't truly know oneself without knowing God. Calvin acknowledged the obvious dilemma in saying, "Which one precedes and brings forth the other is not easy to discern" (*Institutes*, 1.1.1). Knowing yourself is more difficult than one might expect. You might say you are incomprehensible.

YOU ARE INCOMPREHENSIBLE!

Psalm 139:14 says, "I praise you because I am fearfully and wonderfully made; your works are wonderful, I know that full well." Proverbs 30:18–19 tells us, "There are three things that are too amazing for me . . . : the way of an eagle in the sky, the way of a snake on a rock, the way of a ship on the high seas."

We are God's unique creation, and God uses some powerful imagery to describe just how wonderful we are. We are more than wonderful; we are "too amazing" to be grasped. We are incomprehensible!

The Hebrew word translated as "wonderful" in Psalm 139 is the same word that is translated as "too amazing" in Proverbs 30. Psalm 139 paints a picture of the intimate care God gave to our formation in our mother's womb, describing that creation as wonderful. Proverbs 30 gives us a fuller picture of just how wonderful God's creation really is.

To catch the significance of this, try to put yourself into

the mindset of a person who lived around 1000 BC. The scientific revolution had not yet begun, and humankind was 2,500 years away from understanding that the earth is not the center of the universe. Without the scientific explanation for how things happen, this person would have marveled at how an eagle can fly, how a snake can move on a rock, and how a mighty ship can float on water.

Scientists are still discovering how snakes slither forward on smooth surfaces. While they understand much about a snake's locomotion, they are not sure how everything moves together the way it does, the fullness of snake mechanics. It is still incomprehensible!

With all the information we have at our fingertips, it is still "too amazing" for most of us to understand how an 850,000-pound 747 Jumbo Jet can fly. Have you ever seen one of those things land? Watching tons of steel drifting down to earth like a feather is simply too hard to comprehend.

And despite all of our scientific understanding, it is still "too amazing" to imagine how the *Nimitz*-class USS *George H. W. Bush* aircraft carrier floats in the water. The 90,000-ton vessel has more than four acres of flight deck, is twenty stories high, and carries more than three thousand soldiers. Yet it doesn't sink! By contrast, drop one very small rock (you're welcome, all you Monty Python fans) into a pond, and it goes right to the bottom. We find it difficult to conceive how aircraft carriers float.

God says you are just like that.

You are incomprehensible.

It's not because of your abilities or anything you've done. What makes you incomprehensible is your created, God-given potential. And that potential can be realized only when you make yourself available to the Incomprehensible One so he can re-create you in his image, in himself, and spill that re-created you out into others beyond you.

We were created at our conception and experienced physical birth. But those who belong to Jesus have also been re-created in him through spiritual rebirth. Jesus has removed our sense of purposelessness and replaced it with his calling. Jesus invites us to lay down our shallow and self-serving dreams and begin to live out the calling he has for us. He has even cast a vision of what this looks like: "I tell you the truth, anyone who believes in me will do the same works I have done, and even greater works, because I am going to be with the Father" (John 14:12 NLT).

Doing greater works than Jesus did? That *is* incomprehensible! Jesus was a miracle worker. Jesus was a master teacher. Jesus was the world's greatest leader. How can we do works greater than his? The key is that I used the wrong verb tense in the previous sentences. Jesus *is* a miracle worker. Jesus *is* a master teacher. Jesus *is* the world's greatest leader. Jesus works miracles, teaches, and leads through the millions of people he enables to do so today. This is Jesus' plan. Jesus has designed his body, the church, to allow him to incomprehensibly re-create the world through them.

DO YOU COMPREHEND?

There are two types of people in the world. There are those who pursue the joy and challenge of comprehending the incompressible masterpiece God has made them to be, and there are those who do not. Most people fall into the second category, and they live with an aching sense of purposelessness. We see evidence of this all the time. *Fortune* magazine recently featured an article titled, "US Job Satisfaction Hits Its Highest Level Since 2005."[3] And what was that all-time high? A whopping 51 percent. Think about that. A 51 percent satisfaction rate may seem good initially, but that means slightly less than half of us still describe the majority of our day with words like frustrating, dead end, and dissatisfaction.

And when we look even closer, it's even less encouraging. What accounts for this huge surge to the new high of 51 percent? According to the *Wall Street Journal*, higher satisfaction levels reflect declining expectations.[4] More people are giving up and settling. They are resigned to experiencing a degraded sense of dignity and purpose in their work. I'm not sure we can call that progress.

Perhaps one of the most telling proofs of this epidemic of purposelessness is that upper-middle-class, middle-age suicide has spiked 40 percent in the past ten years.[5] The people who are supposed to have everything are growing more disillusioned at how empty everything really is. According to

Psychology Today, "just because a person attempts suicide doesn't mean they want to die. Rather, often they have lost . . . the 'power of hope.'"[6]

But we don't have to live without purpose. And we don't have to live without hope.

No matter how well you understand your calling, there is more for you to realize about your identity as a God-created masterpiece. Where would you put your current level of comprehension in regard to your calling? Ten percent? One hundred percent?

The Bible illustrates for us that God's people have always tended to settle for a low percentage rate, not truly grasping their calling or living out their God-given potential. Behind the following story is a shockingly low level of comprehension. Let's check out the GPS coordinates God gave to Israel about their calling and see how they responded. We start in Joshua 1:2–5, where God gave Joshua this command: "Moses my servant is dead. Now then, you and all these people, get ready to cross the Jordan River into the land I am about to give to them—to the Israelites. I will give you every place where you set your foot, as I promised Moses. Your territory will extend from the desert to Lebanon, and from the great river, the Euphrates—all the Hittite country—to the Mediterranean Sea in the west. No one will be able to stand against you all the days of your life. As I was with Moses, so I will be with you; I will never leave you nor forsake you."

God gave Israel three hundred thousand square miles of land to possess. It was the promised land. But the people had to trust God to receive the promise. It was theirs, but they had to step forward to take it. Sadly, the most they ever possessed was around thirty thousand square miles. Consider that. Out of all the land that God had called his people to possess, the most they ever claimed was a miserable 10 percent.

We could say the people were living out one-tenth of the potential God had intended for them. But why such a low percentage? Maybe they got comfortable with the status quo, and 10 percent felt like enough. Maybe they thought anything more would be a hassle. Maybe it was too risky or costly, so they settled for less than God's promise.

Again, think about your life. How well do you comprehend your calling as a masterpiece created by God? Are you settling for a comfortable minimum? If so, we'd like to make you a promise. We believe that engaging in this journey to find your place in God's story could double, triple, or even quadruple your level of comprehension.

Where do you begin the journey? How do you find your place as an incomprehensible masterpiece and embrace your calling? As mentioned earlier, you need three elements to fully grasp who God has made you to be.

First, you need to know your gifts. Your gifts, talents, and abilities provide the landscape for the work God is creating.

Second, you need to embrace your passions. God has

given you passions for certain causes, people, and purposes. These passions add color to God's masterpiece.

Third, you need to own your story. Your story, even the painful parts, is the canvas on which God is painting.

The first Westerner to see the Taj Mahal was the famous French explorer Jean-Baptiste Tavernier, who arrived at the site in the early 1600s. Finding his way to the masterpiece was no small task. It involved the skills of map reading, navigation, seafaring, foraging, hunting, anthropology, and linguistics. Your journey of discovering and exploring your gifts, passions, and story won't be easy either. We'll provide a framework and get you started, but this will be a lifelong journey of discovery and disappointment. There will be excitement and exhaustion, experiments and failure, break-throughs and impact. But none of this is possible until you decide to set off on the adventure.

Remember, there are two types of people in the world: those who have experienced the joy of comprehending the incompressible person God has made them to be, and those who have not.

Fortunately, you don't need to be Jean-Baptist Tavernier to get started. If you want to find the Taj Mahal today, thanks to the miracle of GPS technology, you can simply look up its location, plot the course, and follow the directions. The journey may still be arduous and time consuming, but you can be confident of the route.

The journey we are inviting you to begin won't have

every step plotted out beforehand, but we will give you a clear direction forward so you can embrace your God-given purpose.

BARRIERS TO LIVING THE INCOMPREHENSIBLE

Many people don't realize that GPS technology was created for military and intelligence purposes. It enabled troops to know where they were in relation to other friendly troops so they could flank and defeat the enemy. GPS technology combined with satellite imagery allowed commanders to have real-time visuals of battlegrounds thousands of miles away so they could make the best strategic decisions. This enabled infantry to target enemy positions without being exposed to enemy fire. The technology is so significant in modern warfare that those without it, or with inferior ways of leveraging it, find themselves at an extreme disadvantage.

What option do they have to level the playing field?

They can jam the GPS signals.

GPS jammers block the signals between the GPS satellites and the GPS instruments on the ground. If there is no signal, there is no intelligence or direction. And if there is no intelligence or direction for the commanders, the enemy can have the advantage.

We mention this because the Bible tells us that we are in a spiritual battle. The GPS we are introducing to you—which triangulates our gifts, passions, and story—is a powerful instrument to help us win the daily battles we face as followers of Jesus. Our spiritual enemy, Satan, knows this and will do everything he can to jam our signals.

I (Brian) have been helping people discover, develop, and deploy their calling for more than a decade. And during that time, I have observed four jamming devices that the powers of evil use to squelch people's ability to perceive their calling. One of the first steps we need to take on this journey is to become aware of the jammers. If you don't know the jammers, you may find yourself experiencing spiritual breakthroughs, only to be followed by significant setbacks. As you read about these jammers, try to determine which of them poses the greatest threat to you. Then share that information with a friend. Give them a call or set up a time to talk, and share what you are learning and why you think this particular jammer could be a problem.

The "Jungles of Africa" Jammer

The first jammer is what we like to call the "jungles of Africa" jammer. Fear is the primary emotion people experience with this jammer. This jammer prevents people from even taking the GPS assessment, for fear it will reveal something they don't want to see. They are afraid of what they might discover, possibly that God wants to send them somewhere they don't want to go, somewhere difficult and challenging.

People who succumb to this jammer's influence fail to recognize that the assessment taps into the passions they already have. In Psalm 37:4, we read, "Take delight in the LORD, and he will give you the desires of your heart."

God may call us to do difficult things, but that's not the full story. As we delight in God, he causes us to desire the things he wants us to desire. When I (Brian) felt God might be calling me to teach, I didn't think I would like teaching. But that was largely because of the context in which I grew up and my limited understanding of the gift of teaching. I didn't realize how much passion I had for it, until I tried it and began to broaden my understanding and gain experience.

If you are truly delighting in God and are surrendered to his leadership in your life, you don't need to be afraid. God loves you, and his Word says that his perfect love drives out all fear. If God calls you to do something, he will be faithful to equip you for it.

The "I Don't Have Anything to Offer" Jammer

The second jammer is what we call the "I don't have anything to offer" jammer. Insecurity is the primary emotion associated with this jammer. People who succumb to this jammer's influence avoid the results of the GPS assessment. They may even give it false information because they believe it will reveal they have nothing valuable to contribute.

This jammer prevents people from recognizing that God is the giver of *all* gifts and that he has given his Spirit to every single one of his followers. His gifts are an expression of his love, his creativity, and his commitment to engage us in his work, and each and every gift and individual involved in God's work matters to God. If you are loved by God, then you are gifted by God, and the gifts he has given you are very special to him!

This jammer is one of our enemy's favorites because it paralyzes those who are afraid of failure. Many risk-averse followers of Jesus use the "I don't have anything to offer" language, believing they can hide behind this wall of false humility. We know because we've used it ourselves!

The key to overcoming this jammer is to understand that we cannot judge the importance of our gifts by the standards of others; we must look at them through God's purposes and plans. What may seem insignificant in the eyes of the world can be incredibly precious to God. Don't underestimate the gifts, passions, and story God has given you to help you determine your calling. God loves you and has a purpose and plan for your life.

The "I'm Too Busy" Jammer

Another common jammer is the "I'm too busy" jammer. Often, ignorance is the primary instigator in this jammer. This jammer diminishes people's ability to see the spiritual and emotional value of engaging their calling. Everyone has the same number of minutes in a day, and how we use those minutes is determined by what we find most valuable. If there is no room in our schedule to discover and develop our calling, then we simply have not valued our calling enough to prioritize it.

I (Brian) am fast approaching the big Five-O. One scary part of this is seeing a growing number of friends and coworkers who are entering their retirement years. Practically every one of my retired friends says, "I'm more busy now than I've ever been. I don't know how I ever had time to work!"

I'll admit that my brain melts down a little when I hear that. First, I wonder if I can get their old job, since it sounds like it didn't take too much of their time. Second, and more serious, I begin to wonder why they can't control their schedule more than they do. What are they doing with all of that time? Does having extra time compel retirees to fill it with more things to do?

I think this tendency reveals something about human nature. We will always fill our time with something, regardless of our situation in life.

Luke writes, in his gospel, about three people who met Jesus along the road and considered following him. Two of the three wanted to follow him but had other things they wanted to accomplish first. One wanted to bury his father. The other wanted to say goodbye to family at home. Now, both of these things are very important! In this instance,

Jesus was asking the two to follow him immediately, perhaps as a test of their sincerity. I believe that in most circumstances, Jesus would have encouraged the people to go and carry out these acts of love. The point for us, as readers, is that there is *always* something very important to do that will compete with discovering, developing, and deploying your calling. It's all a matter of what you value and what is a priority for you.

The "I'm Already Using All of My Gifts" Jammer

Complacency, ignorance, fear, and insecurity can all play a part in jamming our ability to discover, develop, and deploy our calling. There is one final jammer, however, that is found only among those who are using their gifts to serve in their area of passion, and though it doesn't fully jam them, it limits them. It's what we call the "I'm already using all of my gifts" jammer.

My (Brian's) gift of teaching was refined and clarified during my time in seminary. I also had gifts of wisdom and shepherding, and my time in seminary provided training to strengthen those gifts too. Back then, I was certain that these were the only gifts God had given to me, and they served me well in my first church position as a Christian education pastor.

When I left that position to take on another role in helping to transition a church from a traditional style to a more purpose-driven, mission focus, I found that my existing gift mix was inadequate. I was growing frustrated, and my friends encouraged me to use another gift they saw in me, one I didn't see in myself—the gift of leadership. Honestly, any talk of leadership scared me. I was afraid to lead because I was afraid to fail. I didn't know how to lead. I didn't want to learn more about leadership because I was perfectly content using the gifts I had already developed! I even took a leadership ability assessment I found online, and it confirmed what I wanted to hear: I was no leader. The results indicated that I would do just fine as a chaplain for a small group of people and that I would probably never lead a church larger than two hundred people. That assessment gave me permission to rest where I was and not push any farther into exploring the gifts that others saw in me.

God had a different plan.

My friends who knew me well kept pushing me to grow, and I was forced to exercise some spiritual muscles I had never used before. Over time, leadership rose to the top of my gift list. It's one of the gifts I use every day now, and I use it even more than the others.

If you are already using the gifts God has given you to serve him, that's great. But don't close yourself off from additional opportunities. There may be latent gifts within you, gifts that have yet to be called out. It's good to take a fresh look at your life every so often to see if God has given you gifts that you are not fully utilizing.

THE PATH TO INCOMPREHENSIBLE

As you think about the different jammers we mentioned, which one is the greatest threat for you? Which will keep you from getting a good GPS signal? Don't be afraid to name it! We all struggle with one or more of these jammers. But with God's help, we can identify and overcome them and win the battle.

There is land yet to be taken. There are wonders yet to be discovered. You simply need to walk the path.

It's time to get started. Learn your gifts. Understand your passions. Comprehend the story God is writing through your life. And become the incomprehensible masterpiece that God has created you to be.

CHAPTER 2

GIFTS

(Brian) enjoy watching NCAA basketball. And I love March Madness and the crazy stories that emerge from almost every NCAA tournament. If you aren't familiar with the tournament, held every spring, there are four divisions, and each one ranks the qualified teams into "seeds." If your team is ranked 16th, you start off by playing a number 1 ranked team. Good luck!

Since the tournament's inception in 1939, a number 16 seeded team has never defeated a number 1 seed. That is, not until the University of Maryland, Baltimore County, defeated the University of Virginia by twenty points in the opening round of the 2018 tournament. It was the 136th attempt by a 16th seed to defeat a number 1 seed. And against all odds, they succeeded. But they did more than just beat their opponent. They crushed them by twenty points. This was history in the making. *Sports Illustrated*, along with many other media outlets, called the game a David and Goliath event.[7]

Most people are familiar with the tale of David and Goliath. This ancient story has been etched into the minds and hearts of so many that three thousand years after the events themselves, it's a regular part of conversation, even among non-Christians. When I heard television commentators using the David and Goliath story as an illustration of the win, and then later read similar comparisons in several article headlines, it prompted me to wonder what it is about that story that gives it such staying power.

Certainly, there are many factors that explain why the story resonates with us. There is the pervasive influence of the Bible in Western culture, of course. But I believe it goes even deeper than that. I think the David and Goliath story has universal appeal for three reasons: our innate desire to see things made right, our sheer sense of feeling small compared with the things going wrong, and our hope that there is a power that will help us pull off the miracle victory in the end.

In the biblical story, David wanted to see things made right for Israel. David was much smaller than the giant who was threatening his country. And yet David, because of his faith in God, stepped into the battle and emerged with the W. At some level, we all want to be a part of that story!

PLAYING IN THE BIG GAME

In this rest of this book, we will spend a significant amount of time in the story of David and Goliath. Although we will be using this story in a contemporary way, let us first acknowledge that the Bible is always relentlessly connected to its time and place. In this way, the story is written not to us but to a different audience: the people of ancient Israel.

First and foremost, the David and Goliath story is written to capture the theologically interpreted history of Israel for Israel. First Samuel is a part of the Old Testament that explains to the Israelites their origins as an independent kingdom and the emergence of kingship in their nation.

However, just because the story wasn't written *to* us doesn't mean it isn't *for* us.

One of the most important things the New Testament writers help us understand about reading the Old Testament is that a crucified and risen Messiah is the surprise ending to Israel's story. An ending no one expected. That event changed the way the early followers of Jesus read the Old Testament. Postresurrection, the New Testament writers see Jesus as *the* interpretive key to Israel's story. They continually reread and transpose the Old Testament to demonstrate the connection between Jesus and the Old Testament stories. In this view, the Bible is not a series of disconnected stories. It is a single, overarching story in which the stories and characters point beyond themselves to one person: Jesus.

The full meaning of God's story and our story is revealed only in Jesus' story.

What is the ultimate David and Goliath moment?

Calvary! Jesus goes up against the entire sin of the world,

all the forces of hell and death itself. When you and I could not even pick up a stone to win our own salvation, Jesus ran to battle for us and won the battle. In this way, Jesus is the better David. Goliath is evil in all its various forms— sin, demonic evil, and death. We are the fearful Israelites, desperately in need of rescue.

As we rest in that victory won at Calvary and the empty tomb, and when we realize what we have been liberated from, we find ourselves wanting to join the battle to liberate the world from all forms of evil that keep it from all Jesus intends it to be.

None of us are truly free until we are working for the freedom of others.

In this way, we become like Jesus, our David, finding our sling and stones, running to the battle. When we join God to fight that battle, we come alive. In this sense, the David and Goliath story is ours. God has written you into his story, and he is calling you to step up, lean in, and play your part.

In John 10:10, Jesus says, "The thief comes only to steal and kill and destroy." Goliath may be long dead, but there are other giants, impossible enemies that still threaten and taunt us. They are challenging us to a fight, and they want to put an end to Jesus' work on this planet. The battle between David and Goliath is a picture of a larger battle, one that unfolds in the life of every individual. And this story holds two clues for us, Jesus' modern-day spiritual warriors, as we seek to engage Goliath in all of his guises.

Clue 1: The Unlikely Invitation

Clue 1 from the David and Goliath story comes when you answer a question: "How open am I to an unlikely invitation?" Before facing Goliath, David has another encounter, and it involves such an invitation.

A bit of historical background can help. The current king of Israel is a man named Saul, but he's made a series of very poor decisions. He's pandering to popularity and flat out disobeying God's clear commands. So God tells his prophet Samuel, "I'm going to anoint a new king" and sends him out on a mission to find him. By the Lord's leading, Samuel arrives at the house of Jesse. First Samuel 16:6–7 tells us what happens next: "When they entered, he looked at Eliab and thought, 'Surely the LORD's anointed is before Him.' But the LORD said to Samuel, 'Do not look at his appearance or at the height of his stature, because I have rejected him; for God sees not as man sees, for man looks at the outward appearance, but the LORD looks at the heart'" (NASB).

Samuel looks at Eliab, and there is something about his stature that makes Samuel think, "That's the man." He has that celebrity "it" factor. "Look at all the charisma. Of course he's the one to be anointed," thinks Samuel. But take note of what the Lord says to Samuel in response: "Do not consider his appearance or his height, for I have rejected him. The LORD does not look at the things people look at" (v. 7).

This reveals something powerful about how the Lord sees people, how he sees you and me! The Lord is not looking at how many followers you have on Twitter. He's not looking at how perfect your profile picture is. He is not looking at your resume—all the skills and status you've acquired.

Even Samuel, God's prophet, made that wrong assumption. Samuel was a prophet of Israel and had heard God's voice since he was a boy in the house of the Lord, but even he missed what God was up to here. Apparently, he had been so bombarded by resume thinking that at this critical juncture, he couldn't perceive who God was calling. Isn't that sobering? If Samuel missed it, what are the chances that you and I are missing it too? Pretty good, I'd say.

And what are we missing? We're missing God's unlikely invitation.

Samuel says, "Well, Jesse, who else you got?" And Jesse starts bringing out all his other sons, one after another. No lightbulbs go on above any of them. He runs through the entire lineup. Almost.

In 1 Samuel 16:11, Samuel asks Jesse, "Are these all the children?" And Jesse replies, "There remains yet the youngest, and behold, he is tending the sheep" (NASB).

Notice that Jesse says, "Well, there's still the youngest." There is an interesting connotation hidden in the Hebrew word used here. It's not just being the least in age; there's another flavor mixed in. Jesse is saying, "Oh, yeah. There's the runt."

Later in life, David refers to his alienation this way: "I am a foreigner to my own family, a stranger to my own mother's children" (Ps. 69:8). The Hebrew word for strange, *muzar*, is from the same root as is *mamzer*—bastard, illegitimate off-spring. A Jewish tradition suggests that David was, perhaps, an illegitimate son. Regardless of whether this is the case, David was the unlikely candidate, the youngest son, dele-gated to the grunt work of shepherding, one of the lowliest jobs of the day.

But that's not how the Lord saw him. And he made that clear to Samuel, saying, "Arise, anoint him; for this is he" (1 Sam. 16:12 NASB). When David showed up, stinking like sheep, the Lord said, "Rise and anoint him. This is the one" (v. 12). In other words, "I love the runt, the little one, the underdog. My specialty is flipping the tables and doing the unexpected. I'm the God who promotes the pitiful, who transforms the trembling. I'm inviting the unlikely, regard-less of their status and skill."

And that's the heart of God for you! I know that some of you reading this may find it almost impossible to hear such an invitation. Maybe it's the voice of a father or mother, or a teacher or coach. Maybe it's the lies inside your head telling you, "You're not good enough. You're broken. You're dirty. You're nothing."

But that's not what God says to you. God is saying to you, "No. You're the one I'm choosing." Remember, the Bible is not a series of disconnected stories. It is one grand story in which every story points us to Jesus. And while David's anointing was a real event that happened in David's life, it's recorded in

God's Word because it reveals something true for all of us. It stands as a picture of who God uses and how Jesus invites all of us to follow him today. Because of what Jesus has done—his life, death, and resurrection—our worth to him is not about our skills or our status. It is about his grace! And that grace is amazing! That's the good news you need to hear: you're invited. You are the one God wants to use. He has a purpose for you, and he will empower you to fulfill it.

The voices of the resume-thinking, status-obsessed people of this world fill our head with lies, telling us that we don't measure up, that we're the exception to God's ways. Maybe you're a teenager thinking, "I'm too young." David was probably fourteen.

Maybe you feel too seasoned, and you're thinking, "Oh, I'm too old. It's too late to start now." Abraham and Sarah were so old, AARP wouldn't let them in. Maybe you're thinking, "I've done horrible, wicked things. I'm disqualified." God picked a murderer named Moses. He picked a prostitute named Rahab.

Maybe you're intimidated and thinking, "What do I have to offer?" Remember Gideon. He was a frightened farmer. When God called him, he was wearing a pair of Depends, hiding in a winepress. God looked at him and said, "You're a mighty warrior." Does that make any sense at all? It does if you are an expert at redeeming runts. Jesus is *the* pro at human transformation, taking the weak and powerless and using them to accomplish his great purposes.

Are you open to an unlikely invitation? God wants you to know that you are the one. That's the first clue we pick up from this story: we are invited, and it isn't dependent on our status or skill.

Clue 2: The Most Likely Provision

That leads us to clue 2.

Although God's invitation is based on grace and not our abilities, our gifts do play a part in our call. They are inextricably woven into our calling. To understand how these truths fit together, we need to add some nuance here. You have two types of gifts to consider, the natural and the supernatural. We find both of these in David's story.

David was anointed king by the prophet of Israel. That's a huge moment. One would expect something really amazing to happen next! But guess what happens? David walks back to the fields and does exactly what he was doing before—shepherding. The same old same old. Once again, he's another shepherd out on the side of a hill, taking care of the sheep day after day, week after week, year after year. It's not for another four or five years, when the conflict between Israel and the Philistines builds to the Goliath tipping point, that God calls a little guy away from the sheep to take down the big guy.

So what was David doing out there on the hillside all those years? Well, he was learning how to use his sling. Do you remember what David said on the day of the battle? He confidently proclaimed, "Your servant has killed both the lion and the bear; and this uncircumcised Philistine will be like one of them, since he has taunted the armies of the living God" (1 Sam. 17:36 NASB).

David didn't go to Navy SEAL, champion warfare, kill-the-giant, hell week training camp to prepare for his confrontation with Goliath. His training came on the hillside, as he was doing his everyday job. But most of the people don't see this. They don't think David is ready. Just before David goes to the battle, King Saul says, "Whoa. Not good enough. You're not prepared. Let me set you up with some new skills and new stuff."

Saul dresses David in his own tunic, putting a coat of armor on him and a bronze helmet on his head. David fastens a sword over the tunic and tries walking around, because he's not used to these things. Finally, David admits, "I can't go in these."

David is an extra small on the armor size chart, and Saul is a triple-X large. Saul's armor doesn't fit David. It just weighs him down. And David knows it's not going to work. "David took them off. He took his stick in his hand"—a staff that he used while shepherding—"and chose for himself five smooth stones from the brook, and put them in the shepherd's bag which he had, even in his pouch, and his sling was in his hand; and he approached the Philistine" (1 Sam. 17:39–40 NASB).

The staff and the sling. Where did David learn to use these? While shepherding.

In a culture like ours, driven by social media platforms,

microphones, and celebrity status, it's easy to think we can't make an impact when we lack that kind of influence. But microphones, a large social media following, and a stage are forms of Saul's armor. It's easy to think that if we don't have the right speaking skills or can't sing, then we can't really make a difference. But that's not how God wins battles and raises up leaders. That's just Saul's armor.

Don't compare yourself with others and diminish your gifts. Don't settle for Saul's armor. You may need to shift your thinking here. You may not be aware of it, but what you do well—your skills at work or a particular set of gifts you use in a hobby—that's your sling. God has been using your ordinary, everyday activities to prepare you for what is coming next.

God is inviting you to step off the hillside and into the battle. You may not feel like you have the skills needed for the calling. But you know what? God has given you some skills; think of those as your sling. These are the things you naturally do well. Maybe you are good at organizing things, or you have creative abilities, or you are hospitable and friendly. Or you are always ready and eager to serve and lend a helping hand.

This is the question you have to ask: "What is my sling? What are my ordinary, everyday skills?" Maybe you've not connected the dots or even considered that those are the gifts God has given you to take down your Goliath. Ask yourself, "How willing and available am I to use these abilities for the mission of Jesus?"

I (Rob) have a friend named Jamie who leads a fireside

men's group. Every conversation orbits around two questions: "What is Jesus teaching you? What are you doing about it?" A new guy, who'd been attending Jamie's group for six months, began to come alive during those catalytic conversations. And one of the things Jesus awakened in him was a passion to serve the homeless. He'd never done this before, but he began helping out, serving meals down at the Kansas City Rescue Mission. While he was serving, one of the mission leaders learned that he works in IT for his day job, helping install and fix computer systems. The mission leader cried out, "We're in dire need of tech help! Our entire IT system is ancient and faulty."

This man's everyday gifts were exactly what the rescue mission leadership needed. So they asked him, "Can you put down the serving spoon and pick up your sling? We need a geek to slay our Goliath tech problems."

Needless to say, he was blown away. He'd never thought of using his day-to-day skills to serve Jesus. He told the guys at the men's group, "I have this passion to help the homeless. I thought that meant serving meals. But I do IT stuff; that's what I'm really good at. And it turns out, that's what they really need. They need what I'm good at. Now I'm experiencing God's pleasure and direction like never before."

When our day-to-day abilities meet the needs of others, we've taken the first step of running toward battle, armed with our sling. This is what God does: he puts us at the right place at the right time with the right sling in our hand.

I want to ask you to pray this prayer right now: "God, give me ears to hear your invitation. God, give me eyes to see your invitation. Show me my sling and where to run to the battle."

You have natural talents and abilities that God will use to do greater things than you can imagine. But guess what? A sling is not all you have. As with David, God has given you something else as well. We call it your harp. And as we'll see in the story of David, the harp is where God puts his super on your natural, creating a supernatural ability in you.

GOD'S SUPERNATURAL PROVISION

David played an instrument called the *kinnor*, which we translate as "lyre" or "harp." The kinnor had around ten strings, and each string played a different note on what is called the pentatonic scale. David most likely learned to play the kinnor on the hillside or in the fields during quiet moments while he was shepherding, or late at night around the fire, and he was such an accomplished musician that King Saul invited David to play for him. But David's harp playing for the king wasn't for mere entertainment. When David plucked the strings on his kinnor, more than musical notes filled the air. His playing had supernatural power, impacting not only the ears but the hearts and minds of those listening.

We know this because the Bible tells us that an evil spirit was tormenting King Saul. At times, his torment was so intense, he would rage uncontrollably. Not sure what to do, his counselors recommended music therapy, and David was invited to be his music therapist. First Samuel 16:23 says, "David would take the harp and play it with his hand; and Saul would be refreshed and be well, and the evil spirit would depart from him" (NASB).

David's harp playing drove away Saul's demon. We don't know exactly how or why, since the dynamics of the unseen realm cannot be graphed on a chart, and we don't have clear instructions on how all this worked. But the Scriptures do provide us with windows into the interconnected realities of the seen and unseen realms. In this passage, we learn that David's harp playing had an effect beyond the natural. The Spirit of God put his super onto David's natural and created a supernatural ability to drive away demonic evil.

If you've learned how to play an instrument, you might recall your own music making in those first weeks. It likely sounded more like cats in heat than beautiful music. But David had natural ability, and he had spent time practicing in the hills while shepherding, and when his natural gifts met the power of God, something amazing happened. Demons fled. This is a wonderful picture of a spiritual gift—God's power complementing our natural ability in order to accomplish something we could never do on our own. It's God working in and through us in supernatural ways.

Understanding that you have natural gifts is probably not much of a stretch for you. But believing that you have a supernatural ability—that's not something many people consider. Yet the Scriptures are crystal clear: every person who has been regenerated by God's amazing grace, through faith in Jesus Christ and his life, death, and resurrection, is filled with the very Spirit of God (1 Cor. 7:7; 12:4–7; Eph. 4:4–8). And when the Spirit of God takes up residence in us, he brings supernatural gifts and power along with him. The word commonly translated as "gift" in the New Testament is the Greek word *charismata* (Rom. 12:3–8; 1 Cor. 12:4–11, 28–30; Eph. 4:7–12). The word means "gifts of grace," and it refers to the special abilities God has given believers through the Holy Spirit.

You have a harp, just like David. The harp represents your Spirit-empowered abilities, the gifts that God has given you to accomplish for him what you could not do through your own natural strength, wisdom, or skill.

So what is your harp?

Every believer has at least one harp—one Spirit-empowered gift—and when you play that harp, it has a supernatural impact on the hearts, minds, and souls of other people. It changes things in the unseen realm, and that is truly amazing. When you take the online GPS assessment, you will discover that you have both a sling *and* a harp; you possess both natural gifts *and* supernatural gifts.

With that understanding in place, let's take a deeper look at our gifts and abilities.

MAKING IT PERSONAL

If I (Brian) tried to use a sling, I'd probably shoot my eye out. At the very least, I'd break something, and I'm fairly certain I couldn't hurt anyone with it, at least not on purpose. Unfortunately, my lack of ability with weaponry extends to the world of video games. I'm pretty useless when I'm playing a first-person shooter against my boys.

My sons love these games, though, and being a dad who wants to connect with his boys around the things they love, I courageously pick up the Xbox controller from time to time to let them destroy me. Part of my problem is, the new controllers are far more complicated than the old Atari joystick I had when I was younger. Why do you need more than one stick and one button? The controller they use now has two sticks and around ten buttons, and it's all a bit overwhelming. It took me weeks to learn how to move on the screen without bumping into walls or running in circles.

But moving isn't my only problem. Once I had that down, I was quickly overwhelmed by the multitude of weapons, so I asked my sons to limit my choices. That's right. I asked them to make it simple, so I had only a handful of weapons to select from. Faced with a complicated controller and more options than I can handle, I limited myself. My boys still laugh at me for this. They select the very best weapons. Then they upgrade those weapons so they are untouchable, indestructible. And honestly, I can't compete.

But here's the thing. If I didn't limit myself, I'd be over-whelmed. I wouldn't even be able to play the game. And I believe that when it comes to our spiritual gifts and abilities, limiting your options, at least as you are first getting started, is a wise and beneficial strategy.

Picture this. You've been invited to engage in battle against the Goliath of your day. This is not a video game in which the results don't matter. This is a real battle, and the consequences are of eternal significance. But you have been gifted for this battle. You have a sling and a harp.

At this point, you might be tempted to seek out other weapons. David was asked to take up King Saul's armor and sword. I'm sure his brothers had their own suggestions for him too. But one of the keys to David's success was knowing which weapons he could use and which weapons would be a hindrance to him. And in my twenty-plus years of helping others discover their calling, I've found that people experience the most success and have the most impact when they focus on developing and using their top two or three gifts.

They learn to use the sling they've been given. They learn to play the harp in their hand. They understand their natural abilities and learn to develop their spiritual gifts. And this is why our GPS assessment tool is designed to collect information from your everyday life. It's in the context of the day-to-day that you can best determine your primary gifts and abilities. The assessment will provide you with a

FIND YOUR PLACE

short list of gifts and abilities, and this is intentional. Rather than show you every possible way you might be gifted, we give you your top three gift scores and the top three choices in your abilities, to help you narrow your focus.

DEALING WITH THE "BUTS!" AND "WHAT ABOUTS?"

Inevitably, some people are not happy with the results from their assessment. We immediately hear a "But!" or a "What About?" These two responses stem from two different causes.

The "But!" people are unhappy about the gifts that *are* listed. They typically say something like, "But I don't want that to be one of my top gifts!" More often than not, the reason they aren't happy is because they use that ability day after day in their nine-to-five job. I see this often in teachers who take the assessment. They have the gift of teaching and are using it regularly, but not always in a way that is fulfilling to them. There can be several reasons for this, of course. They might be teaching an age group that is not the best match for them. They might be confined by school regulations, and it hinders their joy and excitement. Regardless of the reason, there is something that keeps that gift from being a source of happiness in their work, and they naturally are disappointed at the thought that God might want more of the same, joyless work from them. Sadly, this reaction has

74

kept many people from experiencing the powerful joy that comes when you are using your gifts, empowered by the Holy Spirit, to change lives.

The second response we commonly hear is from the "What Abouts?" These are individuals who are unhappy about the gifts that *are not* listed for them. They say something like, "What about the gift of . . . ?" They are expecting and hoping to see a gift that does not show up. More often than not, this is because they are attracted to a gift they've seen being used powerfully in someone else's life. They see that person's joy and witness the impact Jesus is making through him or her, and they want in on the action! Unfortunately, when this happens, it can be difficult for people to learn to accept their own gifts as valuable.

I remember meeting with a woman who had just taken the assessment and wanted to debrief her results with me. She had both the "But!" and the "What About?" responses at the same time! She was a high-level leader who worked in a large corporation, so it was no surprise to me to see leadership and administration topping her list of abilities. I was excited to review her results and discuss ways she could use those gifts to further Jesus' kingdom work.

I'll never forget the transformation on her face when she saw her results. Her enthusiasm and anticipation quickly turned to disappointment, and she covered her face with her hands. After a few seconds of silence, she looked at me and asked, "What about the gifts of service and mercy? Are those not on the list anywhere?" She was clearly disappointed that these gifts had not shown up.

Soon her expression turned into a grimace that radiated frustration. "I'm tired of using my gifts of leadership and administration! I spend hours and hours away from my family, working endlessly for our higher-ups, and for what? Just to make them more money? I am tired of using those gifts!" I wasn't sure what to say at that moment, so I opted to practice the ever-so-helpful Proverbs 17:28 principle: "Even fools are thought wise when they keep silent; with their mouths shut, they seem intelligent" (NLT).

As I sat quietly, she began to talk, pouring out her heart. With tears in her eyes, she explained how she simply wanted to serve people in a soup kitchen. The results of the assessment made her feel like she couldn't do that, or like she would be betraying God's calling by not using the gifts indicated as hers. But she didn't want to exercise those gifts! She felt overextended in using her leadership and administrative muscles at work and didn't want to do more of that on her "spiritual time." She wanted to feel human again. She wanted to do something that made her feel alive.

I was beginning to see the problem. So I quickly clarified for her that she was welcome to serve any way she wanted! The list was not supposed to limit her. And the humility and compassion she showed toward people in need was a sign that God was doing something in her. If Jesus was prompting her to serve in that way, she needed to follow up on it. But I also reminded her of the principle behind the giving of the gifts. I shared what the apostle Paul wrote in 1 Corinthians 12: "There are different kinds of spiritual gifts, but the same Spirit is the source of them all.... It is the one and only Spirit who distributes all these gifts. He alone decides which gift each person should have" (vv. 4, 11 NLT).

The critical concept for both the "But!" and the "What About?" people to understand is that it is God himself, through the Holy Spirit, who distributes these gifts. And he distributes them *on* purpose and *for* a purpose, and we can trust his discernment. I reminded her that God's Spirit had decided that for her at this moment in time, he had provided these gifts for a reason. Perhaps that reason was still unfolding, but eventually it would be clear. I suggested that she begin serving in the soup kitchen, but that she might also be able to use her leadership and administrative gifts to help optimize the efficiency of soup kitchens around the city and even assist in opening more of them. Immediately the wheels began to spin, and within a few months a new ministry was born.

God himself, through the work of the Holy Spirit, has decided which gifts are yours to receive. This isn't a matter for debate. A spiritual gift is something we discover, develop, and deploy. And none of the gifts are insignificant or less valuable than the others, because they are all gifts of God, given by God, to serve God. The same power that raised Jesus from the dead is ready to be deployed through you, so there is no place for "Buts" or "What Abouts"!

Someone spoke this truth into my (Brian's) life several years ago. My problem was the opposite of the woman's. I had trouble recognizing any gift of leadership in my life. Fortunately, God sent a person at the right moment to speak boldly to me. One of the elders in the church I was serving took me to lunch and gave me a "come to Jesus" talk about my need to step up in leadership. And then he read me a definition of leadership that was different from anything I had considered before. It was an understanding of leadership rooted in the humble, servant heart of Jesus, and it pierced my soul. I still remember this elder looking at me and telling me that I was that kind of leader and that I was responsible to use the gift God had given to me. He made it clear that I was disobeying Jesus if I didn't acknowledge the gift and use it.

I was stunned. But God used him to get my attention.

God, through his Spirit, is the source of all spiritual gifts. He decides who gets them. He knows what he is doing. And he needs you to play your part and stay focused on the gifts he has given.

STAY ON TARGET WITH YOUR GIFTS

I was ten years old when the first Star Wars movie (Episode IV) hit the silver screen. There are several memorable moments in that movie, but the scene I quote most often is when Luke and the other X-wing fighter pilots are speeding toward the Death Star reactor port. One of the pilots, Gold Five, repeatedly urges his team forward despite the threat from the approaching TIE fighters. He repeats the phrase "Stay on target!" over and over again.

I am reminded of that phrase whenever I read the apostle Paul's teaching on the spiritual gifts in 1 Corinthians 12. After listing various gifts and giving the rationale for them, Paul brings his teaching on spiritual gifts to a close by encouraging his readers to stay on target. Paul understood something that we often miss: our greatest strengths can become our greatest weaknesses. When the very power of God starts working through us, it's amazing! Paul wants to make sure that we don't fall into a trap, allowing those gifts to weaken us, so he provides four clear guidelines that will help us stay on target in using our gifts.

1. *Gifts were given to make you helpful, not happy.* Paul starts by reminding us of a key reason why God gives us spiritual gifts: "A spiritual gift is given to each of us so we can help each other" (1 Cor. 12:7 NLT). God, in his infinite wisdom, has made it so that we often experience joy when we use his gifts to serve others. And feeling his power work through us to help others is amazing! But we should always remember that these feelings are a byproduct of using the gifts appropriately. They are not the focus of the gifts. And if

we start to use the gifts for our own gain, to please ourselves, we will begin to experience a decrease in that joy and in the impact our gifts have.

2. *Gifts foster interdependence, not independence.* Paul continues by reminding us that the gifts aren't given to turn us into Lone Rangers. He writes, "There are many parts, but only one body. The eye can never say to the hand, 'I don't need you.' The head can't say to the feet, 'I don't need you'" (1 Cor. 12:20–21 NLT). Jesus is the hero of the story, and he is the only individual who possesses every gift and uses all of them perfectly. The rest of us need the gifts of others working in tandem with our gifts, or the work cannot be done correctly. Like a governor that regulates a vehicle's acceleration, our built-in need for others and their gifts is intended to prevent us from thinking that kingdom work is a solo project. God has designed his gifts to work together!

3. *Gifts are a means to love more than things to love.* Paul makes a swift and powerful transition as he concludes his teaching on the spiritual gifts. He writes in 1 Corinthians 12:31, "Now eagerly desire the greater gifts. And yet I will show you the most excellent way." As he culminates his teaching on spiritual gifts, he entreats us to literally "burn with zeal" in pursuit of them. Then he juxtaposes the role of the gifts with the incomparable value of love. In one of the most

well-known chapters of the Bible, he speaks of love. But his point isn't to highlight a feeling or an experience. It's to remind us that the gifts are not an end in themselves. They are intended to be used to serve others.

4. *Gifts are to be used to their fullest potential.* Perhaps the most important thing we need to remember, though, is the first thing Paul teaches about the gifts. It's also the simplest. He writes, "In his grace, God has given us different gifts for doing certain things well. So if God has given you the ability to prophesy, speak out with as much faith as God has given you. If your gift is serving others, serve them well. If you are a teacher, teach well. If your gift is to encourage others, be encouraging. If it is giving, give generously. If God has given you leadership ability, take the responsibility seriously. And if you have a gift for showing kindness to others, do it gladly" (Rom. 12:6–8 NLT).

Notice that with each gift he mentions, Paul urges the person who has that gift to use it wholeheartedly and with excellence. It's a simple reminder that gifts are meant to be developed and used to their full potential. Think about the opportunities you have to develop your abilities. You can read about spiritual gifts and connect with others who are using their gifts. If you aren't sure where to start, try asking your pastor or your church's discipleship director to help you identify others with gifts similar to yours, so you can learn from them. Share your top gifts with your coworkers or neighbors—people you interact with on a daily basis—and as you use your gifts to serve others, ask them to give you feedback. Ask if your service is blessing them or if there are ways you can grow and improve. But more than anything else, start using your gifts! You do not need to be a ready-made expert. You don't need to get it right every time. You just need to start using your gifts and trusting God to do his work through you.

SLING AND HARP: HOW DO THEY DIFFER?

Earlier, we looked at the story of David and how we each possess certain natural gifts, and we observed that as followers of Jesus, we each have supernatural gifts as well. But how do these differ?

If you recall, we referred to our natural abilities as our sling. These are your first order gifts. They are first order because they show up first in the biblical narrative, and they also show up first in your narrative. When you were born, you came out with natural aptitudes. You'll often hear parents remark on how incredibly different their children are. "This oldest just took to athletics naturally. But our youngest, they were always more artistic." I had a friend who could hum in harmony with the refrigerator by the time he was three years old! As you can imagine, no one sat down and taught him how to do that. You won't be surprised to discover he is a professional musician today. Of course, nature and nurture interact dynamically. You have to develop those natural aptitudes, but we're all born with them.

These natural gifts are the product of God's common grace, given to all people. Common grace is a theological term used to describe the goodness of God to all humankind universally (Acts 17:25; Ps. 145:9; Matt. 5:45). One of the aspects included in common grace is the set of natural gifts and talents we were born with (Ps. 139:13–16; Gen. 1:27; James 1:17).

That takes us to the creation narrative. Genesis 1:27 tells us, "God created mankind in his own image, in the image of God he created them; male and female he created them."

You are the handiwork of God himself, created in his image. The divine image you bear includes the gifting God has woven into you. You were knit together by God, and you are fearfully and wonderfully made (Psalm 139).

Those gifts are given with a purpose. Genesis 1:28 puts it this way: "God blessed them and said to them, 'Be fruitful and increase in number; fill the earth and subdue it. Rule over the fish in the sea and the birds in the sky and over every living creature that moves on the ground.'"

Our natural abilities come with an invitation to co-create with God—"fill the earth and subdue it"—so there will be order and flourishing in the world. Theologians have titled this co-creating and ordering work the "cultural mandate." Nancy Pearcey, in her book *Total Truth*, explains what this means: "The first phrase, 'be fruitful and multiply,' means to develop the social world: build families, churches, schools, cities, governments, laws. The second phrase, 'subdue the earth,' means to harness the natural world: plant crops, build bridges, design computers, and compose music. This passage is sometimes called the Cultural Mandate because it tells us that our original purpose was to create cultures, build civilizations—nothing less."[8]

The cultural mandate is about creating things of value that add to the flourishing of the world in every corner of culture. And to do this, we rely on our natural abilities. When we use these abilities, we honor God by joining in this purpose for humanity: to create and add value to this world. The job description shows up clearly again in Genesis 2: "Now the LORD God had planted a garden in the east, in Eden; and there he put the man he had formed. . . . The LORD God took the man and put him in the Garden of Eden to work it and take care of it" (vv. 8, 15).

God started the garden project and invited his kids to join him. Why did he put them there? To work. In essence, he said, "This garden is a gift. Your natural abilities are a gift. Work is a gift. Get to work using your gifts in the garden!" Our gifts aren't ultimately about us getting a paycheck or feeling like we're better than someone else because they aren't as good at something as we are. Using your natural gifts is a noble part of your calling to join God in co-creation, and it has great intrinsic value.

That's why God gives us slings.

But followers of Jesus have something more than a sling. We referred to this as a harp, a supernatural, spiritual gift. You might call these second order gifts, not because they are less important but because they are something we have in addition to our natural, created abilities. They show up second in the biblical narrative and in our narrative as well.

The Bible is not just the story of creation and the call to co-create; it is also a story of redemption from sin and evil, which has marred the cultural mandate. As you know, shortly after the cultural mandate was given, our earliest parents chose to rebel. A counternarrative enters the story.

At the tree of the knowledge of good and evil (Genesis 3), shame, fear, and alienation are introduced into the human condition. A rupture has opened up at the core of every individual; shalom is torn apart *within* us. We no longer live at peace with ourselves. Even worse, we no longer live at peace with God. Next, this rupture rips into our personal relationships; shalom is torn apart *between* us. As the story progresses, the first murder (Cain and Abel, Genesis 4) shreds the precious gift of community. By the time of Noah (Genesis 5–8), the mean streets of society are filled with violence and corruption. And when we finally reach the Tower of Babel (Genesis 11), we have an evil empire, and the trajectory of this civilization is genocide.

In essence, we are now working uphill because of the entrance of sin and rebellion. The problem isn't just "out there," in culture and society, but in us. We will never be able to fulfill the cultural mandate without a divine intervention that can save us from sin and transform us from the inside out. What we need is a new creation! The first order has been corrupted. We need a new beginning and a second order! A new identity! A new nature! A new community!

Jesus came to give us all of that. He came to save us, and then he sent us into the work of this new creation.

When Jesus rose from the grave on Resurrection Sunday, something new began. In the midst of a fallen world, stained with sin and suffering, Jesus brought something new. This morning was the birth of a new creation. The first creation had been marred by the fall, and the human race was barred from the garden of Eden. But the alienation, condemnation, and corruption that entered the world in that first garden, God reversed in the garden tomb. Jesus rose from the dead to begin a new creation week, remaking the world and restoring all things.

One day, long ago, the first man was made from the earth, and his rebellion led to death. But on Resurrection Sunday, the God-man, the Lord Jesus Christ, came up out of the earth with resurrection power, conquering sin, death, and hell, both now and forevermore. And his resurrection leads to life eternal.

In a clever twist in John 20, Mary mistakes Jesus for the gardener of the tomb-filled garden. And though she is wrong about his identity, she is right in calling him a gardener.

The One who planted the first garden in Eden is now planting a new garden, the church. This garden isn't about religious events and services and buildings; it is a movement of people transformed by his grace and power who have surrendered their life's agenda to join his mission of redemption and restoration. This is the second order.

Fundamentally, the work of redemption and restoration, the work of the second order, is a work that must be Spirit empowered, because no amount of human effort alone can cause spiritual transformation. The ability to do this work in the second order is secured through the life, death, and resurrection of Jesus Christ and empowered by the Spirit, whom Jesus sent to us following his ascension.

It is by grace we have been saved and brought into this second order. Paul proclaims in Ephesians 2:8–9, "It is by grace you have been saved, through faith—and this is not from yourselves, it is the gift of God—not by works, so that no one can boast." In Christ, the work of salvation is *done*, so we don't have to do it. Because it is done, we can now enter the new creation, the second order, and the new humanity Jesus has embodied and initiated by grace. You must choose to accept this gift of grace. With that choice, you are born again (John 3:1–18; 1:12). You join the church via your adoption as a beloved child of God.

As the church, we aren't just saved from something; we are saved for something! What is that? Paul pivots to that in verse 10: "We are God's masterpiece. He has created us anew in Christ Jesus, so we can do the good things he planned for us long ago" (NLT).

Jesus summarizes the mandate for his church with these words: "Go and make disciples of all nations, baptizing them in the name of the Father and of the Son and of the Holy Spirit, and teaching them to obey everything I have commanded you" (Matt. 28:19–20).

This is where we need our harps—our supernatural abilities. Jesus has given spiritual gifts for the church mandate: to multiply disciples and fill the earth with his followers. These second order gifts are given at our second birth, when we are born again by the work of the Holy Spirit. Paul says in 2 Corinthians 10:3–4, "Though we live in the world, we do not wage war as the world does. The weapons we fight with are not the weapons of the world. On the contrary, they have divine power to demolish strongholds."

Our natural abilities can create wonderful things, but it is through our spiritual gifts that we discover a divine power to make disciples, strengthen the church for her mission, fight demonic evil, and fully manifest the kingdom. Through the Holy Spirit and our spiritual gifts, God empowers his church to bless the world at large.

The ultimate vision of the new creation is not that we fly away to the sky in the sweet by and by. Quite the opposite: the ultimate vision is that the kingdoms of the world become the kingdom of our Lord (Rev. 11:15). God comes here. We don't go to him. God makes the kingdoms of this earth his kingdom. Jesus' ultimate vision is not about getting you and me to heaven but about getting heaven down here through us (Matt. 6:10). The kingdom of God will infiltrate and transform this world. The cultural mandate and the church mandate finally merge.

"Then I saw 'a new heaven and a new earth,' for the first heaven and the first earth had passed away, and there was no longer any sea. I saw the Holy City, the new Jerusalem, coming down out of heaven from God, prepared as a bride beautifully dressed for her husband. And I heard a loud voice from the throne saying, 'Look! God's dwelling place is now among the people, and he will dwell with them. They will be his people, and God himself will be with them and be their God. "He will wipe every tear from their eyes. There will be no more death" or mourning or crying or pain, for the old order of things has passed away.' He who was seated on the throne said, 'I am making everything new!'" (Rev. 21:1–5).

The kingdoms of this earth will become the kingdom of our God. God's rule and reign will be fully manifested. Unlike the corrupted, oppressive, dehumanizing, and enslaving empires of our world, the empire of Christ will be benevolent, good, humanizing, and liberating.

Jesus' vision was summarized with these words: "the renewal of all things" (Matt. 19:28). Everything broken made whole. Everything sick healed. Every blind person given sight. Every prisoner set free. Every injustice vanquished. Jesus' mission will not be complete until every people group in the world has received the good news, in both word and deed (Matt. 28:18–20; Luke 24:46–49; Rev. 7:9). Jesus' mission will not be fulfilled until the world is fully restored, a place of universal flourishing. The Bible describes this ultimate reality as the new heaven and the new earth.

One day, we will be living, loving, working, relating, and reigning with Jesus in a resurrected version of this world. A place where shalom is finally realized and everything is as it ought to be. What God intended from the beginning will be fully revealed.

One day, people from every tribe will join God in co-creation, new work in every field of human endeavor. People from every tribe will join him in managing and steward-ing this world, but without the hindrance of war, violence, and scarcity—a world without tsunamis and famines, and without the hindrance of our own internal brokenness and selfishness.

For as John the Beloved said in 1 John 3:2, "What we will be has not yet been made known. But we know that when Christ appears, we shall be like him." Right now, as followers of Jesus, we have this constant internal tug-of-war between our new nature in Christ and our broken, sinful nature. In that day, we will be free because our old nature will be redeemed and healed. We will freely choose what is good and wise and right and holy and beneficial, all the time. What we see in Jesus now we will see in ourselves without hindrance.

We can't get there on our own; we need the power of the Spirit, and we wait for the return of Jesus, who will finally judge and vanquish evil. But it's our mission to bring that future into the present, to make the kingdom tangible everywhere, to proclaim the good news throughout the world, to see disciples of Jesus fill the earth with mercy, justice, love, truth, and beauty.

One day, we and all of creation with us will fully become God's masterpiece.

Wow! We get to be part of all this! How?

One way is by using your sling (natural gifts) and your harp (spiritual gifts) to work toward that end. Can you see how much knowing your natural gifts and spiritual gifts matters? They are integral to you participating in both the cultural and church mandates. Our slings and harps differ in their focus and ability, but they are both important. The table on page 92 gives a quick summary of how natural gifts and spiritual gifts differ.

What's the significance of all this for understanding your calling? Practically, it means you need both your sling and your harp in order to play your part in this massive plan to see God's redemptive love fill the world.

Hopefully, the first signal in identifying your calling is now clear—your gifts, including your natural abilities and your spiritual gifts. But that's not all you'll need. That's only the beginning. To fully triangulate your calling and find your place, you'll also need the next signal—your passions.

The Difference between
Natural and Spiritual Gifts

Types of Gifts	*Natural Gifts*	*Spiritual Gifts*
Source of Gifts	Common grace (grace given to all people regardless of their belief)	Saving grace (grace given to those who choose to place their faith in Jesus Christ)
Origin of Gifts	At birth and through intentional development	At second birth when the Spirit takes up residence within the new believer
Receiver of Gifts	All people	Followers of Christ
Intent of Gifts	Participation in the cultural mandate: bringing order to culture and adding value to the world through work	Participation in the church mandate: making disciples, strengthening the church, and making the kingdom of God tangible in service
Orientation of Gifts	*First order: creation.* We work in the world for the purpose of cultural flourishing so that every area of society will thrive now.	*Second order: new creation.* We also work toward the world to come—the new heaven and the new earth—through the advancement of the Great Commission and the renewal of all things that will be realized at the return of Jesus.

CHAPTER 3

PASSIONS

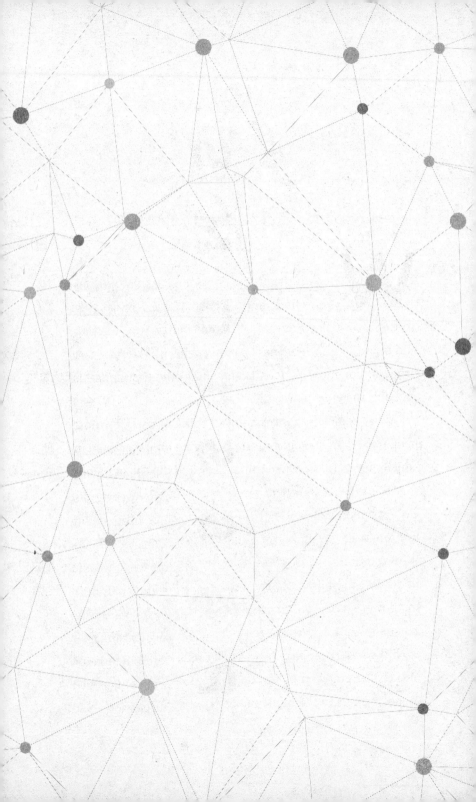

We are in the process of triangulating three signals to find our place, our unique calling in life. To do this, we need to understand our gifts, our passions, and our story. Each of these signals helps in the discovery process. For most people, the second one—passions—is probably the most powerful.

What comes to mind when you think of passion? Most people think of strong feelings, of having an experience in which they feel alive, when things click and they have a sense that this is what they were made to do. As we discover our God-assigned passions, we will begin to shift from feeling lost and confused to gaining clarity about our place in life. While our gifts outline some of that direction, when we add in an understanding of our passions, we begin to tap into the power source that motivates us to pursue our calling. This is essential, because the pursuit of your calling isn't always going to be easy or simple. God's call may take us into challenging and difficult situations. We're being called to a battlefield in the midst of a war, and our passions help us understand why we are fighting and provide the why that empowers us to remain at our post, even when things get costly and dangerous.

The Bible tells us that each one of us is born into a world at war—a spiritual war that has existed since the beginning. Jesus regularly addressed demons, sending them away, liberating those who were under their influence. The writers of the New Testament go to great lengths to describe the different kinds of corrupt cosmic agents that have rebelled against God and now exercise an oppressive and damaging influence over this world. With terms like "rulers," "powers," and "authorities" (Rom. 8:38; 13:1; 1 Cor 2:6, 8; 15:24; Eph 1:21; 2:2; 3:10; 6:12; Col 1:16; 2:10, 15), "principalities" (Eph. 6:12 NKJV), "cosmic powers" (Eph. 6:12 NRSV), "spiritual forces" (Eph. 6:12 NASB), and "elemental spirits" (Col. 2:8, 20; Gal. 4:3, 8–9 NRSV), they are describing a massive conflict that is far deeper and more profound than we can fully comprehend. When we face giants like poverty, disease, illiteracy, and sex trafficking, it is not just human dysfunction at play but also systematic demonic evil. We are called to liberate people in slavery to their addictions and sinful desires, through the power of the gospel. God commands us to speak his truth to those who are spiritually lost, to rescue them from the oppression of demonic influence.

Like young David, we face a great enemy who far surpasses our strength and abilities. But we also have a crucial role to play in slaying these Goliaths. God asks us to step up to the fight, to engage the battle, and to rely on him to defeat these enemies. When we don't walk in faith and clearly understand our passions, we end up ignoring our responsibility. We're like off-duty, drunken sailors, fighting each other rather than keeping our focus on the real enemy. If we fail to man our passion-revealed battle station, we will end up fighting the wrong people and the wrong battles.

Talking about battles reminds me (Rob) of what my family now refers to as the wet wipe warmer incident.

Shortly after Christmas in 2003, my youngest daughter, Belle, was born, and soon after mom and baby returned from the hospital, I was sent out on a mission: to buy a new wet wipe warmer. Our old one had died and was no longer warming the wipes properly. If you've had children, you know that a baby's job description consists of only three things: eating, pooping, and (hopefully) sleeping. As a father and husband, I figured the least I could do was provide the proper equipment to make the pooping part of that job as painless as possible.

Soon I found myself standing in the checkout line with a wet wipe warmer. A woman pulled up behind me, her cart jammed full of Christmas clearance items. In it were more than a dozen Santa hats, several of those reindeer antler thingies (she was sporting a pair), scores of little chocolate Santas, and sundry holiday goods.

Peeking over my shoulder, she looked at the package in my hands and asked, "What *is* that?"

Thinking I would be applauded as Super Dad, I smiled. "It's a wet wipe warmer for our new baby."

At this, the women scrunched up her face, then came out from behind her cart. "Let me see that," she said, grabbing it from me. She turned it over in her hands, locked eyes with me, and indignantly screamed, "What is *this* for!"

I could tell she was annoyed, but I wasn't sure why, so I explained. "It's a wet wipe warmer. It warms up wipes, so they're not ice cold on the baby's bottom."

She looked at me incredulously. "This is the most obtuse appliance I've ever seen!"

If I had known what the word obtuse means, I probably would have been offended.

Now, remember, this all happened while I was standing at the checkout counter. The checkout guy was waiting to scan the item, and the line behind us was beginning to grow. It was getting a little awkward. But the woman was oblivious to the scene she was creating. Continuing in her mocking tone, she began criticizing my wife. "I suppose Mom can't just take a towel and dip it in some hot water? She could do that, or you could buy this convenient wet wipe warmer for nineteen dollars and ninety-five cents!"

I exchanged a glance with the checkout guy, who now had a frightened look on his face. I wondered if he was considering pushing that little red emergency button under the counter.

"I suppose that it has to be plugged in all day, every day,

just burning up electricity," she said. "I wonder how much that adds to your electric bill each month." She closed her tirade repeating her earlier statement. "The most obtuse appliance I have ever seen!"

At that point, I wasn't sure if she was just really Dutch, passionate about eliminating frivolous costs, or was a fringe environmentalist looking for ways to reduce energy usage at any cost. Or maybe she was just a crazy lady wearing reindeer antlers. We may never know.

I was dumbfounded. Taking the item back from her, I mumbled to myself, "Yep, it keeps the wet wipes warm." The clear irony of her wearing fake reindeer antlers and purchasing tacky Santa hats never clicked for her, and I was too afraid to mention it. But it still bothers me.

What does all this have to do with finding your passion and locating your calling? I mention it because this was a woman who had passion in her, real passion. She was clearly passionate about the wrongness of wet wipe warmers and was ready to battle it out with a complete stranger. And that's my point. When we aren't tapped into the real battle—the battle that matters—we tend to fight battles over things that don't matter. And we end up fighting the wrong enemies. You see, we all long for something worth fighting for. And we were created by God to fight, to love what is good and seek justice in this world. You and I were made to slay giants, and God calls us to step into the battle. But how do you know which battle to fight? How do you determine which enemy to engage?

It's our passions that show us where and who we are made to fight.

The Israelites had been in a long-term standoff against the Philistines. For nearly two hundred years, the Philistines had harassed and oppressed the Israelites, often invading their territory and at times threatening their very existence. David's older brothers were recruited for the fight. They are on the front lines. David's father calls David—too young to be involved in the battle—in from the fields and asks him to take supplies to his brothers. But when David arrives at the battlefield, he finds something surprising. His brothers aren't fighting. No one is engaged.

In the ancient world, two nations or tribes would sometimes engage in champion warfare. A champion would be chosen from each nation, and they would go man-to-man as representatives fighting on behalf of their people. The Philistines picked their biggest, baddest dude—Goliath. He was their champion. First Samuel 17:3–7 gives us this description: "The Philistines stood on the mountain on one side while Israel stood on the mountain on the other side, with the valley between them. Then a champion came out from the armies of the Philistines named Goliath, from Gath, whose height was six cubits and a span. He had a bronze helmet on his head, and he was clothed with scale-armor. . . . The shaft of his spear was like a weaver's beam, and the head of his spear weighed six hundred shekels of iron; his shield-carrier also walked before him" (NASB).

This wasn't the first time God's people faced an enemy. Generations earlier, the first man and woman had faced another adversary armored in scales—a serpent who sought to turn their hearts from their loving Creator. And God's people would face other enemies after this. In David's story, we see reflections of the larger story, the story of God's people facing down their enemy, battling against all that is evil and corrupt in this world.

For context, it helps to understand some of the shaping forces and values of Philistine culture. The Philistines paid homage to Dagon, their god of fertility, by offering children as sacrifices, even burning them alive. The burning of children should remind us of similar atrocities, such as the concentration camp of Auschwitz, lynchings in Mississippi, or recent reports of children in Europe being sold from orphanages so their organs can be harvested. Connect the enemies of God in David's story with the evil we face today. When you think of girls being sold into brothels in the sex traffic industry, think of Goliath. When you think of children dying from diseases that could be prevented with a twenty-five-cent shot, think of Goliath. When you think of innocents being slaughtered by religious radicals with suicide vests, think of Goliath.

Whenever you think of injustice in all of its various forms, think of Goliath.

Because while sin affects each of us individually and we must deal with it individually, it also has systemic effects.

Sin can gather a head of steam across cultures and generations until it becomes an entire system that oppresses and marginalizes people. Think of the systemic sins we battle today, sins of racism, disease, poverty, ignorance, illiteracy, and others. Goliath has many names.

We've domesticated Goliath and made him a friendly, motivating metaphor for our warm, fuzzy personal goals. Goliath is not about me getting my next promotion or my kid winning their next soccer game. Goliath is about something so much bigger.

There is an epic battle between good and evil that goes far beyond our personal goals for success. And God is looking for some unlikely candidates, like David, who are willing to say, "God, I want to get in on the battle." When David arrived on the battlefield, he asked the men standing near him, "What will be done for the man who kills this Philistine and takes away the reproach from Israel? For who is this uncircumcised Philistine, that he should taunt the armies of the living God?" (1 Sam. 17:26 NASB).

David sees the battle and is ready to fight. He could have chosen to focus on his own plans or spend time working on his own goals. He could have said, "I've got a full schedule. I've got my hands full already, caring for my father and his portfolio of sheep. I've not been trained or equipped for this scenario. Perhaps I could make a small donation toward a fund that would provide for the soldiers? Or perhaps there's a small volunteer role I could take on, an hour per week?"

Instead David embraced the challenge and, trusting God, said to the Philistine, "'You come to me with a sword, a spear, and a javelin, but I come to you in the name of the LORD of hosts, the God of the armies of Israel, whom you have taunted. . . .' Then it happened when the Philistine rose and came and drew near to meet David, that David ran quickly toward the battle line to meet the Philistine" (1 Sam. 17:45, 48 NASB).

Notice that David ran toward the battle. He saw a problem, he sensed the injustice, and something within him rose up to fight it. David looked at Goliath, his passions awakened, and he said, "That's all I can stand, and I can't stand no more!"

And that begs the question, what is your passion? What battle are you running toward? Where do you sense a problem, an injustice, a wrong that needs to be righted?

What is the name of your Goliath?

This is really important. It's worth taking some time to probe your heart, to ask yourself what you are willing to fight for. What are the issues that awaken your heart, because in that awakened set of passions is an invitation from the living God to join him on his mission. So before we forge ahead, we'd like you to stop and consider this question of passion in more detail. We find it helpful to break down the question into three areas: your people passion, your cause passion, and your influence passion. As we discover and explore these aspects of passion, we learn the name of our Goliath and how to recognize which battle we are called to run toward.

YOUR PEOPLE PASSION

There are certain groups of people that you naturally care about. Something in your story causes them to be of special interest to you. This is your people passion. Here are a few questions that can help you uncover your people passion.

1. What group of people do you intuitively care about?
2. To whom has God sent you? What group of people do you sense God moving you toward for the purpose of his mission?
3. To what group of people can you be a missionary? Missionaries move in and become one with the people in a particular culture; which people do you think God has called you to "move in" and "become one" with?

Discovering your people passion starts with an understanding that the God we serve is a missionary, and by his very nature, our God is a sending God. We see this most clearly in the mission of the Son of God, whose passion and love for his rebellious people was so strong that he left his throne in heaven to embark on a costly mission to redeem them. Mission is not simply an activity God participates in; it is a reflection of his nature, an expression of his divine love, the overflow of his glory.

The loving heartbeat of God radiates from the Father,

through the Son, into the Spirit-filled church, and it empowers us and sends us out on mission to the world. As God sent Israel to be a light to the nations, and as the Father sent the Son, now the Father, Son, and Spirit send us, the church, to bring God's good news and love to a lost and broken world. As followers of Christ, we are a sent people! And what began in the heart of God now flows through our heart toward people in our environment. That's the essence of your people passion. It's a yearning to redeem and restore that which is lost and broken. It's the heart of the Good Shepherd looking for that lost sheep. It's God's "No Child Left Behind" policy.

God's mission will have as many different manifestations as there are different people. For some, participating in that mission will mean spending time with disadvantaged children, reading to them after school, or coaching a team or mentoring a teen. For others, it will mean reaching out to the neighbors, having them over for a meal or a movie, hearing their story, and finding ways to serve and encourage them. It might mean spending time with seniors in nursing facilities, some of whom are left alone because of broken relationships. Or working to stop human trafficking, by informing people of influence or by serving in a women's shelter. For still others, it means serving a cup of hot soup and a sandwich to a homeless person on a cold day.

You get the picture. There are as many manifestations of people passion as there are people with needs in this world. To whom has God sent you?

When you choose to serve others, you begin with involvement in their lives, but over time that shifts toward identification. Consider the example of Jesus, who in the incarnation became one of us, identifying with us in our sinful condition and serving us in our great need for a Savior. Eugene Petersen describes it this way: "The Word became flesh and blood, and moved into the neighborhood" (John 1:14 MSG).

Jesus didn't send us an email offering us salvation or stop by for a brief visit. He moved into the neighborhood and lived with us, loved us, served us, suffered with us, and died for us. Are there people whose needs awaken a special passion in your heart? We are called to be like Christ and get involved to the point of identifying with those God wants us to love and serve. Over time, we move from "them" to "us" and "we."

I (Rob) have a friend named Josh who was enslaved to a porn addiction for many years. Through the help of a support group and the training he received there, Josh has been living free from his addiction now for many years. And in place of that wrong desire, he now has a white-hot passion to come alongside others who are facing the same addiction he struggled with. He is passionate about helping men who are oppressed and about bringing healing to their families. When Josh starts talking about this, his conviction is clear: "I just can't stand to see another marriage or family destroyed by this addiction!" You can feel the heat coming off his soul.

Josh is leading a support group at the church where I serve, and he recently began work on a master's degree in counseling. When I look at Josh, I can sense his passion for men and their families, and I can picture the countless lives that will be transformed as he pursues his people passion.

Josh has found his place, his calling. And his passion was one clue to locating it.

I also think of Brian and Kristen, a married couple with five kids. Brian and Kristen heard the voice of Jesus when he said, "Love your neighbor as yourself." They immediately knew he wasn't just speaking metaphorically; he was calling them to love their neighbor. As a pastor, I've found that many followers of Jesus fail to live out their mission in their own neighborhood, but I think Brian and Kristen are a great example of how to do this right where you live.

Brian and Kristen have begun thinking of themselves as little church planters in the neighborhood where they live. They throw parties for their neighbors, they organize loving acts of service, and they have created a safe place on their porch, at their kitchen table, and by the grill in their driveway, where folks in their neighborhood can talk about spiritual matters. Many of Brian and Kristen's neighbors have decided to follow Jesus. This couple has also had an impact on scores of other believers. They've inspired other couples and families with similar passions to start church communities in their neighborhoods and through their relational networks. Imagine how the spiritual landscape of a city might change if every Christian were equipped to live with this kind of people passion!

That's GPS in action, right there. Brian and Kristen have found their place. And their passion for people helped them find it.

One final story. Whitney was on a mission trip last year to serve the disabled, and she experienced a burning bush moment in which Jesus spoke to her soul. "*This* is what I want *you* to do," he said. "Serve the disabled." A passion was born in her heart that day, and Whitney now spends Sunday afternoons with Gunner, an autistic student at her school, making the love of Jesus tangible by simply being his friend. She's also exploring colleges, looking for one that will best equip her to be an advocate for the disabled. Imagine how many future Gunners will be loved and equipped because of one young woman who is faithfully stewarding her people passion. And by the way, that young lady is my (Rob's) daughter!

That's GPS in action, right there.

So what is your people passion? Who do you have a burning passion to love and serve?

YOUR CAUSE PASSION

You discover your cause passion by looking at the issues or causes that you naturally feel drawn to. These causes captivate you, and you find yourself researching them in your spare time. Here are a few questions that can help reveal your cause passion.

1. What group of causes lights you up?
2. What issue of injustice makes you want to run to the battle?
3. If there was one area in which you could make a difference, what would it be?

There are many causes in the world, so many broken places, oppressive policies, and empty philosophies that strip humans of their God-given dignity. Evils like poverty, slavery, and racism are fault lines shaking the foundations of our society with regular tremors and occasional quakes. Jesus helps us to pinpoint the source of these tremors. Speaking of the devil, the ancient enemy of humanity, he says, "The thief comes only to steal and kill and destroy" (John 10:10).

We've talked about the damage that old enemy continues to leave in his wake. He came as a lying serpent, he challenged God's people through a Philistine giant, and he continues to work his evil plans, seeking to steal, kill, and destroy all that is good in this world. But Jesus provides the solution to these challenges: "I have come that they may have life, and have it to the full" (v. 10).

Jesus came to make all things new, and as he says here, he came to give life where the enemy has brought death. And not just a weak taste of life but life to the full. As followers of

Jesus, we bring a message and engage a mission, doing battle with the slings and harps he gives us.

The mission of God is a mission of blessing and redemption, of standing against injustice and advocating for those in need. A man named Moses is called to lead God's people out of slavery, and he proclaims these words about God: "He defends the cause of the fatherless and the widow, and loves the foreigner residing among you, giving them food and clothing" (Deut. 10:18).

Later, in Deuteronomy 27:19, we read this: "Cursed is anyone who withholds justice from the foreigner, the fatherless or the widow."

God's people are liberated from their own slavery to be a light to others. A redeemed people, they are called to a ministry of redemption for others, and one of the predominant indictments the Old Testament prophets had against Israel and Judah was their failure to provide this type of justice for the oppressed. The prophet's words in Amos 2:6–7 are as relevant today as they were thousands of years ago: "The people of Israel have sinned again and again, and I will not let them go unpunished! They sell honorable people for silver and poor people for a pair of sandals. They trample helpless people in the dust and shove the oppressed out of the way" (NLT).

After Amos shares the countless ways the Israelites have ignored or exacerbated the injustices in their land, he powerfully shares this declaration from God himself: "Let justice roll on like a river, righteousness like a never-failing stream!" (Amos 5:24).

When Jesus arrives on the scene, his life and ministry fulfill the promise given to Abraham, bringing blessing in a variety of ways. While Jesus met our spiritual need for liberation from sin, restoring us to God, he also modeled for us how to serve the sick, the imprisoned, the hungry, the forgotten, and the disrespected. Jesus' treatment of women, foreigners, the lame, the possessed, and even the blind and the rich serves as an example of how we are to live our lives. Jesus told us a parable of how God will one day separate the people of the world into two groups: the people who met the needs of others, and the ones who did not. The ones who saw the causes and met those needs were his true sheep whose actions revealed that they belonged to him. The ones who ignored those causes were called goats and were sent into eternal punishment (Matt. 25:31–46).

In the decades after the ministry of Jesus and the start of the church, the apostle Paul, following in Jesus' footsteps, regularly received an offering for the poor. James, with words reminiscent of those of Moses, drove home the need for actions that match our salvation and point to the one who saved us: "Religion that is pure and undefiled before God, the Father, is this: to care for orphans and widows in their distress, and to keep oneself unstained by the world" (James 1:27 NRSV).

God, from the beginning of the Bible until the end,

has been redeeming his people and then challenging and empowering them to address the brokenness of the world.

This is a second form of passion—a passion for a particular cause, a longing to address a specific injustice or wrong. You don't have to be a pastor or serve on the staff of a church. You simply need to identify your cause passion and then step up to do battle.

We understand that it can be overwhelming as you consider the multitude of causes in the world. Here is a short list of some causes in the world where Goliath has been picking a fight.

- Families/marriage
- At-risk children
- Abuse/violence
- Financial management
- Divorce
- Disabilities
- Law and/or justice system
- Sanctity of life
- Homelessness
- Recovery
- Prison inmates/families
- Illness and injury
- Sexuality/gender issues
- Education
- Policy and/or politics

- Race relations
- Business/economy
- Relief efforts
- Ethics
- Health and/or fitness
- Science and/or technology
- Environment
- International affairs
- Community/neighborhood

Which of these causes inspires you to go into battle and fight? Are there others, not on this list, that resonate with your heart? Take a moment to think about this. It's important to name the cause where Goliath has declared war as specifically as you can. When you know the kinds of people you want to fight for, and you understand the cause you want to uphold, the final clue to identifying your passion is understanding how you can influence the fight.

YOUR INFLUENCE PASSION

The third and final aspect of passion is your influence passion. This is a little different from the earlier two, in that it speaks to the manner in which you can best unleash your passion. In order for you to identify it, you need a bit of biblical background. We'll start with Ephesians 4, where the apostle Paul speaks of believers and the church. "To each one of us grace has been given as Christ apportioned it. . . . Christ himself gave the apostles, the prophets, the evangelists, the pastors and teachers, to equip his people for works of service, so that the body of Christ may be built up until we all reach unity in the faith and in the knowledge of the Son of God and become mature, attaining to the whole measure of the fullness of Christ" (Eph. 4:7, 11–13).

Writing about the various equipping offices of the church, Paul highlights five roles that correspond to the fivefold mission of the church. For our purposes here, we'll refer to these as "influencing styles" because they reflect different ways in which the passion of God is mediated through his people.

The combination of these five influencing styles creates an unstoppable force for unity in the church, building up the body and helping us all to become mature in our character and calling. To remember the five styles, the acronym APEST is helpful.

- Apostle
- Prophet
- Evangelist
- Shepherd
- Teacher

These five styles are not just leadership roles that reflect the calling of a few individuals; they are lifelong influencing styles given to every follower of Jesus. Only Jesus fully lived out all five to their full potential. And all of us can grow in all five of them. But each of us has one style that is primary among the five. Here are brief working definitions of each of the APEST gifts.[9]

- The *apostle* sends and extends. These are people who are tasked with the extension of Christianity as a whole, primarily through missions and church planting. The apostle (from the Latin term meaning "sent one") is a person who is on a mission of being sent, and those who have the apostolic style influence others by emphasizing the work of sending and multiplying.
- The *prophet* questions and critiques. These are people who feel called to maintain faithfulness to God among the people of God. Prophets are guardians of the covenant relationship, calling out sin and challenging God's people to greater fidelity to God, his Word, and his ways.
- The *evangelist* invites and gathers. These are people who influence by recruiting others to the cause, who love to share the gospel and proclaim the truth about Jesus. They are naturally infectious and able to enlist people in the movement through their communication and actions.
- The *shepherd* protects and provides. These are people called to nurture spiritual development, maintain communal health, and engender loving community among the people of God.

- The *teacher* explains and organizes. These are people who mediate wisdom and understanding. This philosophical style of influencing others brings comprehensive understanding of the revelation bequeathed to the church.

Author and pastor Mike Breen suggests that it might be helpful to think of the five ministry areas from A to T along a continuum.[10] At one end you have pioneering or entrepreneurial types, and on the other you have builders and developers. The apostolic and prophetic types will land more toward the pioneering end of the continuum, the evangelists will typically land somewhere in the middle, and the shepherds and teachers will be more toward the developer side of the continuum. This is because the apostolic types will have a tendency to try new things, exploring the frontiers, while the teaching types will be more comfortable building on the base that is already developed. Here is what you need to remember: we need folks across the entire spectrum in order to function well.

If there had been no pioneers in the United States two hundred years ago, we'd all be stuck on the East Coast. But if developers had not come after the pioneers, building solid cities and communities, we'd never have grown beyond our limits as a nation. It required different people with different gifts and roles to work together.

Apostles send and extend. And they will be the most

likely candidates to protect that value. The apostles are on the forefront, working on the frontiers and exploring the edges of what is possible. They're drawn to design, thinking about the overall system, and they have a missional focus. You could describe them as adventurous and futuristic, and when they're leading from their strength, they are decisive and strategic. They're concerned about answering the question, "Will this help increase our mission?" They contribute to team environments by laying new foundations, and they are not afraid to push boundaries. When their style is out of balance or immature, they can come across as driven, demanding, and insensitive.

Prophets question and reform. They're sensitive to God and what's important to him, they have a love for what is true and right, and they know what needs to be emphasized when it comes time to challenge and confront. The prophet asks questions and can sometimes be a provocateur, deconstructing and critiquing the current systems and structures. Their strength for the movement is their strong intuition of right and wrong. They also have a tolerance for mystery and embracing the unknown. Their leadership style will be demonstrative and motivational. They're looking to answer the question, "Will this help embody God's concerns?" They anchor the movement in God's values and help realign when the team (a church, a group on mission, a work group, a family) is out of sorts. Negatively, this style can tend toward being ideological, shortsighted, and simplistic.

Evangelists recruit and gather. These folks love meeting new people and wooing them into relationship. They're great communicators and are most often very convincing. In regard to the team, they are relational and communal, with an emphasis on novelty. When leading from their strengths, they are motivational and persuasive. The evangelist is trying to answer the question, "Will this help us bring people to the point of conversion?" They explicitly value the gospel story and have an ability to share that story in everyday ways with everyday language. In a negative light, they may appear to be willing to do anything to make the deal, and they might be seen as not demanding enough.

Shepherds protect and provide. They have a natural instinct to protect the community from danger and provide for its needs, both communally and individually. They're drawn to nurture the communities they lead and focused on healing and wholeness. Their leadership style is inclusive and collaborative. The shepherd seeks to answer the question, "How will this affect the organization and people in the community?" They contribute to the team by cultivating relationship and integrating people into a socially cohesive network that fosters relational growth. The negative side of the shepherd can manifest as an obsessive need for harmony and an aversion to risk.

Teachers understand and explain. These people find great satisfaction in helping others learn truth and wisdom. They tend to be more philosophical and find it easier to grasp complex systems and truths. They have an ability to help others understand, and they emphasize curiosity and learning. Their leadership style is analytical and prescriptive, and they try to answer the question, "How does this line up with theology and Scripture?" They are natural trainers, good at systematizing and articulating truth. When someone operates out of the shadow side of this gift, they will be ideological, seeking conformity, and they may lack urgency when it is required.

APEST FOR DUMMIES

We have a friend named Dan who owns a few Dunkin' Donuts stores in Wichita, Kansas. Dan is a smart guy, smart enough to know that he needs the input of different kinds of leaders to keep his business thriving. Dan is also smart enough to know that every consultant he talks with about his stores has a different opinion on what is most important. One consultant might look at Dan's network of stores and advocate growth, the need to start more stores and expand to locations in Salina, Manhattan, Hutchinson, and beyond. This type of consultant is a bit of an entrepreneur, focused on new startups to improve the business. In our APEST classification, we would call this person an apostle.

Another consultant might want to do a thorough inspection to make sure Dan's stores are up to the best company standards. She would inspect the facilities for cleanliness, check the sales and business records for accuracy, emphasize a dress code for employees and training for proper customer relations. Her approach could be seen as that of a district manager. In our APEST classification, we would call this person a prophet.

A third consultant might encourage Dan to come up with creative ways to get more customers. He would emphasize the need to develop the brand, refine the message so it is clear and convincing, and develop brand loyalty. We would probably call this a marketing approach. In our APEST classification, we would say this person is an evangelist.

A fourth consultant might begin by going straight to the customers, walking through the stores to see that customer needs are being addressed. He might spend time talking to the staff to see if they are checking if customers need refills, if the climate controls are adjusted to customer satisfaction, and if employees are wishing customers a wonderful day. This is the customer relations approach. In our APEST classification, we would call this person a shepherd.

The final consultant might focus on the policies and procedures, making sure they are up to date and the employees are well informed. He might schedule seminars or training sessions to better equip employees in their work, or a special seminar to dig into the why behind the what of the policy manual. This is a training approach, and in our APEST classification, we would call this person a teacher.

The point of this illustration is to show that the styles are broadly reflective of different approaches to organizational leadership. Each consultant brings a different perspective and offers his or her diagnosis of the problem and a unique set of solutions. And while each approach has valid insights, the real benefit comes when they are considered together as a whole.

So what would your primary agenda be if you showed up at one of Dan's stores? (Aside from eating all of Dan's donuts.) What's your consulting instinct? Would you be most interested in extending the business? Would you want to make sure the business is focused on doing things correctly? Would you be trying to help Dan recruit more customers? Would you be concerned about improving the customers' welfare? Or would you focus your time and energy on training and better equipping Dan's employees?

The answer to this question will help you determine your influencing style. And this is important to know, because you will often bring that style to your passion as you seek to meet the needs of people or serve the cause you are passionate about.

PRIMARY AND SECONDARY INFLUENCING STYLES

We hope you find the concept of influencing styles helpful. There is one additional aspect of this concept that is important to understand. We all have a primary and a secondary influencing style. Your primary (or dominant) influencing style will be fairly obvious, because it reflects your motivation—what drives your passion. Your secondary style will often be reflected in your means—how you seek to accomplish what you are motivated to do, the way in which you express your motivation. I (Rob) am an apostle teacher, which means that my foundational motivation is apostolic, but the primary way I express that apostolic motivation is through my teaching. I have a friend who is an evangelist shepherd. This means he is primarily motivated to share the good news with those who don't yet know how much they matter to Jesus. He will challenge his faith community to be witnesses and redemptive agents in their vocations and neighborhoods. Secondarily, as a shepherd, he will express this evangelistic motivation not by teaching or preaching but by caring for people and developing meaningful relationships. As you can see, there are many combinations of primary and secondary styles. Knowing your primary and secondary influencing style will give you even more clarity about your passions.

It is also important to remember that although we all have a primary influencing style, it does not mean we are locked into that style. We can certainly learn to function in the other four styles as well. After all, Jesus perfectly influenced in all five styles, and our desire should be to become more like Christ, seeking to serve as many people in as many different ways as God allows us to. As Jesus lives in and through us, we have the potential to use all five styles. It's unlikely that we will ever fully develop all five, because God has created us with limitations. He wants us to live as a body, interdependent and aware of our need for each other. But opportunities occur, for a season of ministry or in a time of crisis, when we may need to learn how to function in a style that is different from our primary influencing style.

Hirsch and Catchim have done some wonderful work developing this concept, and they put it this way: "Not everyone is an apostle, but all of us are called to live on mission. Not everyone is a prophet, but everyone needs to know how to listen to God. Not everyone is an evangelist, but we're all called to share the good news. Not everyone is a shepherd, but everyone is supposed to care. Not everyone is a teacher, but we're all called to share what we know."[11] The bottom line is that we each need the impact of all five influencing styles. Furthermore, the health of any church or team is contingent on all five of these styles operating synergistically.

In your body, there are nine different systems. You have a circulatory system, a respiratory system, a central nervous system, a skeletal system, a digestive system, and so on. When these nine systems are all in balance, the body is healthy. And when a body is healthy, life and growth happen naturally. Just ask the parents of any healthy kid. You can't keep them in shoes for very long. They keep growing too fast! Anytime one of the systems in your body gets out of balance, you have a disease, and at that point you head to the doctor. The task of health-care professionals is to diagnose where you are out of balance and advise you on how to bring your body back into balance so all the systems work together again.

In Ephesians 4, "Dr. Paul" describes the body of Jesus, the church. He explains that we have several systems in the body. We have an apostle system, a prophet system, an evangelist system, a shepherd system, and a teacher system. All of these systems work together to keep the body in balance, leading to health and growth in the body of Christ.

God has big plans for this body!

Dr. Paul tells us that God's plan for his body is for it to grow until it fills the entire world with the presence of Jesus. But for that to happen, all five systems need to be in balance. What does this mean for us? First, it means that it's important for you to discover and embrace your influencing style and learn to live it out. Second, it means that we are interdependent when it comes to our spiritual health and wellness. We must remember to value and champion all five influencing styles in every team, every group, every effort, and every church.

If this is your first encounter with the concept of APEST, we encourage you to pick up the brief book *The Permanent Revolution Playbook* by Alan Hirsch and Tim Catchim. Alan and Tim's concepts have been very helpful for many leaders, and we believe that the concept of influencing styles is one of the keys to understanding and fully leveraging your God-given passions for God's glory.

FUSION: THE POWER OF COMBINING GIFTS AND PASSIONS

It is time to bring the David and Goliath battlefield into the twenty-first century. It's time to talk about *fusion*.

For all you non-geeks out there, nuclear physics tells us that fusion is what happens when the union of atomic nuclei form heavier nuclei, resulting in the release of enormous quantities of energy. If that sounds like Greek to you, here is the key concept. Things combine together, uniting, and energy is released. Lots of energy.

What does this have to do with what we've been learning? Well, identifying and understanding your gifts—your sling and harp—is a powerful thing. And it's powerful to identify the Goliath that God has called you to confront. Amazing things happen when you identify the people, the cause, and the influencing style behind your God-given passions.

But what happens when you join those two things—your gifts and passions?

You get fusion, a reaction that unleashes an awesome form of energy.

This is the energy that mobilizes followers of Jesus to run

into battle with the confidence of David. It brings purpose and passion to those who have burned out and feel empty. It awakens the sleepy believers who have never stepped out of their comfort zones. And it satisfies our thirst to indulge our passions, in godly rather than ungodly ways. Fusion of gifts and passions drives us from within instead of motivating us with threats of punishment, guilt, or manipulation.

Imagine the energy that could be released if the 2.2 billion followers of Jesus on earth today experienced such a fusion reaction. Imagine that world for a moment. It's the power of Jesus leveraged to share the love of Jesus, all to accomplish the shalom of Jesus.

I like the world I see there, a world where artists render the beauty of God's creation, medical personnel meet needs on a global scale, and philosophers and ethicists inform political policy, leading to the end of poverty. Teachers empower and encourage their students. The kingdom would come and God's will would be done, on earth as it is in heaven.

WHICH PASSION WILL WIN?

We began this chapter with the wet wipe warmer incident. Man, that woman had passion! The problem, however, was that her passion was misplaced. She's a perfect example of the maxim "If we do not allow God to master our passions, our passions will master us."

Experience has taught me that most of the pain in our lives is caused by our pursuit of ungodly passions. Passion is a powerful thing, and our passions can drag us to the edge of a cliff and push us over if we fail to channel them in godly and productive ways. The good news is that God has freed us from being mastered by our passions, and his Word gives us a guide to mastering them.

One of the best ways we know to illustrate this concept is to describe how a groom feels when his bride-to-be comes walking down the aisle. I (Brian) was so taken by my wife's beauty, delighting in her, that I would have done anything she asked of me. I was weak-kneed and ready to serve her, regardless of the request.

Delighting in Jesus means loving him and putting him first in our lives. We are captured by his beauty, his wisdom, and his sacrifice on our behalf, and that melts our hearts, making us ready to serve him, regardless of the request. We delight by abiding, listening, and learning from him. Delighting in Jesus is allowing him to call the next play in your life.

Psalm 37:4 tells us that as we delight in Jesus, he will give us the desires of our hearts. And lest you think we're taking a verse out of context, Jesus validates this truth in John 14:13–14: "You can ask for anything in my name, and I will do it, so that the Son can bring glory to the Father. Yes, ask me for anything in my name, and I will do it!" (NLT).

Jesus says he will do anything we want. But he adds

that there is a purpose behind his granting of our prayers and requests: "that the Son can bring glory to the Father." When we share in Jesus' passion to glorify God, he is ready to empower us by answering our prayers and meeting our needs. The key to unlocking the power of Jesus is found in sharing the source of Jesus' delight—pleasing the Father. Elsewhere, Jesus tells us that he must complete the work the Father gave him to do. He must speak only the words the Father gave him to say.

Jesus delighted in his Father, and the Father acted on his behalf. When we act on the desires Jesus gives us, the Father is glorified and we share in the delight and joy of God.

TAKE THE ASSESSMENT!

So here is where we've come so far. We hope you have a better awareness of the gifts God has given you—a combination of natural abilities and spiritual gifts. And we hope this chapter has opened your eyes to your passions—your people passion, your cause passion, and your influence passion. At this point, you may be wondering, "What do I *do* with all of this?"

Well, as helpful as it is to know this material, if you want to receive the full benefit of this book, you need to take the next step and apply it to your life. And the simplest way to do this is to take the free GPS assessment. If you have not taken the assessment yet, you can do so at *www.giftpassionstory.com.*

So that's the next step. Finish this chapter, put the book down, visit the website, and take the gifts and passions portions of the assessment. Most people are able to finish those two portions in less than thirty minutes. As you will see online, we encourage you to stop after taking the first two portions, in order to review your results. We'd also encourage you to read chapter 4 (the next chapter) before proceeding with the story portion of the assessment. There we will prompt you to look back through your story before you start looking ahead. Please be patient with the process! We know that many of you are ready to go, but the real benefit of the assessment comes when you understand how the results fit together. Remember, that's the power of fusion!

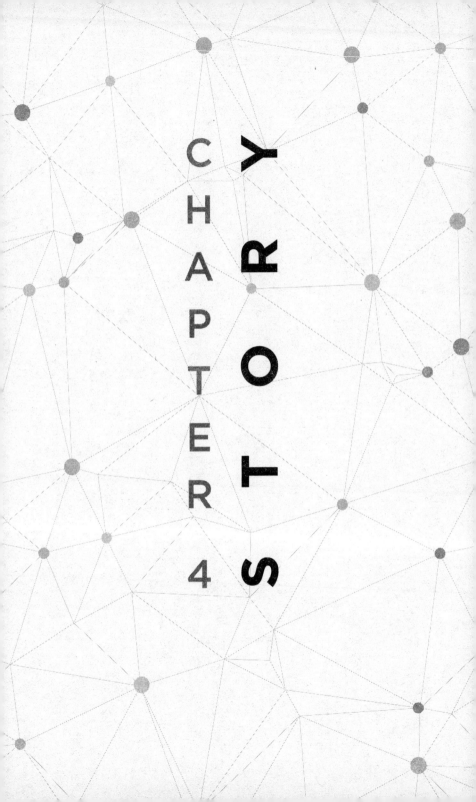

CHAPTER 4

STORY

odern technology isn't perfect, but all things considered, it's a wonderful and amazing gift. Earlier, we talked about the GPS technology that is now commonly used in our smartphones, in our computers, and in countless other ways we often don't realize. One of the most common ways is still the driving app, a simple program that guides us to a destination. If you lack a sense of direction, there's always that soothing voice to tell you everything will be okay. You are on the right track! Just drive two miles, then turn right. And if you miss the turn or make a wrong one, your GPS will gently guide you back. "Recalculating. Turn around." Finally, when the journey ends, you are rewarded with those affirming words "Arriving at destination."

But life doesn't always work out that way, right?

Maybe you've heard of or experienced a GPS failure. You carefully follow the step-by-step instructions, only to realize that you've been taken to an empty field or an abandoned building on the wrong side of town. If you need a few laughs, google "GPS failure" and read some of the stories.

- "I ended up down a dirt road, that turned into a two-track in the woods. Which then ended at what can only be described as 'murder cabin' in the woods!"
- "I plugged in the address for the funeral parlor. The GPS took me to a junkyard. It felt like the GPS was trying to teach me some obscure life lesson I couldn't quite figure out."
- "A twenty-three-year-old drove one hundred feet into a freezing Ontario lake Thursday night after sticking too closely to her car's GPS directions. . . . She was uninjured but had to swim back to shore."

The last story is from a news article with a photo of the car submerged in the bay! GPS fail is funny when it yields a humorous anecdote. A delay in getting to a destination is frustrating, but most of the time it isn't a matter of life and death.

But the kind of GPS fail we are talking about can be tragic when it means someone is missing out on their one-of-a-kind calling. By this point, we hope you are tuning in and increasing your reception of the three key signals for locating your calling—your gifts, passions, and story. These signals are essential to finding your place in life. When you triangulate them, they guide you toward a clearer sense of purpose and direction.

The first two signals we've explored together have largely been internal readings, focusing on your abilities, talents, motivations, and passions. But this final signal is more external. It involves learning to read and interpret the details of your life journey, your unique story.

The apostle Paul tells us, "Clearly you are an epistle of Christ . . . written not with ink but by the Spirit of the living God" (2 Cor. 3:3 NKJV). Paul says that we are living letters being written by the Spirit of God. How does that work?

In Christ, the plot points of your life culminate in a narrative that shapes who you are. Your story isn't just a list of facts and events. It's a weaving of those facts and events into a narrative that has meaning, one that connects with God's larger story. When you listen to the details of your life with your ear attuned to the Spirit, meaning emerges. A life story doesn't just say, "Here's what happened." It also says, "Here's what matters." Your story illuminates who you are, what the events of your life mean, and who you are becoming, and it all points toward what will happen next.

There is an arc to your story. Do you know how to read it? There are themes to your story. Are you aware of them? Most of us don't take time to reflect on our story. And even when we do, we are so enmeshed in our story that it can be difficult—virtually impossible at times—for us to perceive its patterns and meaning. We desperately need the perspective of the Letter Writer to guide our understanding and interpretation.

We believe that the best way to move ahead in discerning your calling is to look behind into your story. You have to look backward to go forward.

One of my favorite movies is the Chris Nolin neo-noir thriller *Memento*. The genius of this film is that it weaves together two narrative sequences, one that runs forward in black and white, and one that runs backward in color. The color sequences are shown in reverse chronology. The main character, Leonard Shelby, is trying to solve a mystery, searching for the people who attacked him and killed his wife. But Leonard also suffered trauma from the assault, and he now has anterograde amnesia, the inability to form new memories. This means he suffers short-term memory loss every five minutes. To compensate, he creates an intricate system of "memory" using polaroid pictures and self-made tattoos. The two narrative sequences, one forward and one in reverse, meet up at the end of the film, when you have one complete and cohesive narrative that finally makes sense. And as the story runs in reverse, as Leonard pieces the clues together, the murder mystery is solved.

LOOKING BACK

So what clues should we look for as we look back at the events of our lives? The clues to your calling can be divided into two categories: your brokenness and your blessedness. What do we mean by this? Simply that meaning emerges through your suffering and your success, through your pain and your progress.

Let's look at an example of how this works, in a story from the Bible. In one of my favorite Gospel stories, Jesus is walking with two unnamed disciples on the road to Emmaus. This is in the days following his resurrection from the dead, but the disciples don't know yet that he is Jesus. What should have been incredibly obvious—"We are walking with the resurrected Son of God!"—was veiled to them.

Luke simply records, "Jesus himself came up and walked along with them; but they were kept from recognizing him" (Luke 24:15–16).

Jesus asks them a simple question: "What are you discussing together as you walk along?" (v. 17). The disciples describe for Jesus the events of the previous week, how Jesus had done powerful miracles, how they had hoped he would bring redemption to Israel, but instead he had been betrayed by the leaders and crucified. Then they drop this bombshell: "Some of our women amazed us. They went to the tomb early this morning but didn't find his body. They came and told us that they had seen a vision of angels, who said he was alive. Then some of our companions went to the tomb and found it just as the women had said, but they did not see Jesus" (vv. 22–24).

Well, if a man who has raised dead people says he will come back to life, and you find an empty tomb, maybe you're missing the nose in front of your face! It appears that this is how Jesus felt. His next words can only be called a smackdown: "'How foolish you are, and how slow to believe all that the prophets have spoken! Did not the Messiah have to suffer these things and then enter his glory?' And beginning with Moses and all the Prophets, he explained to them what was said in all the Scriptures concerning himself" (vv. 25–27).

They had the facts of the story, but they didn't understand how those facts fit together. They assumed a certain conclusion—that the mission of Jesus had failed—and even though there was a missing body, they could not yet understand how the facts pointed to an alternate narrative. It wasn't until later, as they were sitting around a table, sharing bread with Jesus, that their eyes were opened and they could piece it all together. Luke records this moment: "When he was at table with them, he took the bread and blessed it, and broke it, and gave it to them. And their eyes were opened and they recognized him" (vv. 30–31 RSV).

In the blessing and the breaking of the bread, they recognized Jesus. This story serves as a paradigm for how Jesus brings understanding to our story. As we sit with Jesus, he brings blessing and breaking, and we learn to recognize him. It's as we look to Jesus through our blessings and our brokenness that our eyes are opened to see him. Just as he gave new meaning to the events of Israel's history and his own suffering, he intends to give new meaning to the events of our lives.

There is one other helpful lesson hidden in this passage. Just before the meal, when all was revealed to the disciples, there was a pivotal moment on which their experience of this revelation depended. "As they approached the village to which they were going, Jesus continued on as if he were going farther. But they urged him strongly, 'Stay with us, for it is nearly evening; the day is almost over.' So he went in to stay with them" (vv. 28–29).

We don't know why Jesus was dropping hints that he intended to keep going. But as we study Jesus elsewhere in the Gospels, we learn that he often asked people questions to test their commitment, their level of desire. "What do you want me to do for you?" "Do you wish to be healed?" In this case, it seems likely that his hint at moving on was an offer, an invitation with a question for the disciples: "Do you want more? Do you want to understand? Do you want me?"

Jesus was giving them an opportunity to prove their passion. Are you a passionate seeker or just a casual inquirer? Are you a fan or a follower? These are questions we need to ask ourselves, because God will bypass men and women who don't realize their need for him, who have it all figured out and don't recognize their ignorance. He isn't interested in using those who are self-sufficient. Rather than passionately seeking Jesus and strongly urging him to stay, they settle for casual inquiry into his mission.

Think about how you would respond to Jesus. Are you content with your own understanding of your story? Have you considered that Jesus may be writing a different story, providing fresh meaning to the events of your life? We encourage you to take some time to reflect on your blessings and your brokenness. Come to Jesus with a heart of humble dependency and gracious urgency. Only he can bring the revelation you need; only he can interpret your story for you. Pray and ask him to open your eyes to see his purpose for you.

As you reflect on your story, you may want to break it up into seasons. Start with your childhood, then focus on your youth, and then, depending on your age, ponder the events of early adulthood, middle age, and your senior years. What have been the defining moments? The turning points? What events have been difficult for you to understand? How has God brought blessing, even in times of brokenness and pain?

Erik Reese, in his book *S.H.A.P.E.: Finding and Fulfilling Your Unique Purpose for Life*, says, "Imagine yourself walking down a long hallway. On the walls are paintings that reflect those life-shaping moments in your life. On one side are portraits of experiences that brought you excitement, achievement, and fulfillment. On the other side hang pictures of experiences that caused pain, frustration, and remorse. Walking slowly down the hallway, looking carefully at each painting, is an important step toward understanding who God created you to be and discovering your Kingdom Purpose he has set aside just for you."[12]

If it helps to picture yourself walking down that hallway with Jesus, do so in prayer, reflecting on the blessings of your childhood, youth, young adulthood, middle age, and senior years. Take note of the moments of blessing that were meaningful to you. And remember that just because a moment was insignificant to someone else doesn't mean it wasn't significant to you. I (Rob) clearly remember an incident in the fifth grade when I tried out for the concert band. The band director, Mr. Beamer, had each of us experiment with different instruments: brass, woodwinds, percussion, and others. As I finished the percussion tryout, Mr. Beamer exclaimed, "You're a natural drummer!" No one had ever told me I was a natural at anything, ever! I remember how my heart lit up at those words, and that moment ignited in me a passion for music that still burns today, almost forty years later. That event influenced me in my late teens and early adulthood, as I would spend hours banging drums and playing loud guitars. Eventually, I became a worship leader, arranging music and coaching teams to lead an entire congregation to encounter Jesus through music.

I'm pretty sure the band director doesn't remember that moment, but it's one I'll never forget. What moments are especially meaningful for you? Consider some of the following blessings from my (Rob) story.

- *Vocational accomplishments.* Example: I started my first business in fifth grade, selling my inventions at school, and I still start new things all the time.
- *Academic successes.* Example: I graduated magna cum laude, and that academic bent has shaped me to be a teacher and author.

- *Relational achievements.* Example: My family has multigenerational holiday traditions that we savor and pass on.
- *Spiritual breakthroughs.* Example: From my youth, I've had a string of personal experiences with Jesus that are the milestones of my journey, each profoundly informing how my life influences others.

As you think about God's blessings in each area in your life, consider the momentum that resulted from each event, how it continued to affect your life. Try to put into words any meaning you have attached to the event. Early in the great story we read in Scripture, God says to Abraham, "I will bless you . . . and you will be a blessing" (Gen. 12:2). God blesses us so we can be a blessing to all people. This means that our blessings have a missional momentum. What has been the trajectory of your blessings? Ask Jesus to open your eyes to see him. Ask him to interpret those elements of your story. Record your thoughts and reflections.

The next part will be a bit more difficult.

We want you to walk that hallway with Jesus again, except this time notice the portraits of brokenness. As much as we value our strengths, it is often in our brokenness that we discover the ways that Jesus will use us most profoundly. When we share our strengths, people benefit and they are grateful. But often people will look at our strengths and say to themselves, "I could never do that." Teaching is one of my

(Rob's) strengths and, by God's grace, often has an impact on the lives of others. But I know that many people in the congregation will watch a gifted teacher and say to themselves, "I could never do that!"

When we share our brokenness, though, people are more inclined to think, "I can relate to that." The good news revealed in the gospel is that Jesus never wastes our pain; he recycles it for a new use. When we grasp this, the events of life take on a whole new meaning. Paul speaks of how our troubles can be used by God to bring comfort to others in their trouble and suffering: "Praise be to the God and Father of our Lord Jesus Christ, the Father of compassion and the God of all comfort, who comforts us in all our troubles, so that we can comfort those in any trouble with the comfort we ourselves receive from God" (2 Cor. 1:3–4).

We've all experienced hurt. We have habits and hang-ups. We have regrets. We all have something we are recovering from, whether that is abuse, bullying, cancer, divorce, addictions, depression, job loss, bankruptcy, the death of a child, a miscarriage, the suicide of a loved one, a dysfunctional family—the list goes on. As you walk the hallway with Jesus, observe the portraits of brokenness as you reflect on the seasons of your life. Recall personal, vocational, relational, educational, and spiritual places of pain. Touch each of those portraits, remembering that no matter what happened, Jesus can renovate and revive a marred portrait. He can recycle what has been damaged.

We typically think of recycling as something we do with cans and magazines. But the word recycle literally means "to adapt to a new use." In the past few years, it has become popular for people to take old furniture, clothes, and even broken appliances and find fresh applications for them. An old desk can be recycled with a fresh coat of paint. A broken toy can be transformed into a new work of art.

In a similar way, Jesus recycles our regrets by adapting them for a new purpose. And as creative as some people can be at turning old bottle caps and pieces of garbage into works of art, none of that can come close to the creativity and brilliance of Jesus. He is a master craftsman, recycling billions of regrets into masterworks of art. What was useless becomes useful. What was broken becomes beautiful. Paul writes, "We know that in all things God works for the good of those who love him, who have been called according to his purpose" (Rom. 8:28). This is the greatest recycling project in history. No matter what you put into Jesus' recycling bin, he can adapt it for a new use.

As you contemplate your portraits of brokenness, ask yourself, "How has Jesus met me in my pain, and how can I reach out to others in that same kind of pain? How might Jesus recycle my pain for his purpose?" Who can better help an alcoholic than somebody who has struggled with alcoholism and is now living sober? Who can better help somebody dealing with the pain of abuse than someone who was abused and has done the work toward healing? Who can better help somebody who lost their job and went bankrupt than somebody who lost their job, went bankrupt, learned from it, and began again? What is the trajectory of your moments of brokenness? Ask Jesus to open your eyes to see him. Ask Jesus to interpret those parts of your story. As you do this, record your thoughts and reflections.

ESTABLISHING THE HIGHLIGHT REEL

Psalm 139:16 tells us that even before we were born, God was already at work writing our story: "Your eyes saw my unformed body; all the days ordained for me were written in your book before one of them came to be." All the days of our lives were written in God's book. That simple yet powerful statement rivals Psalm 23 in helping us understand and trust in the shep-herding heart of God. Regardless of your theological views on questions like predestination, this verse is a personal message from God, a reminder that he knows you better than anyone. He is aware of everything, every day of your life. He was there to celebrate with you on your happiest day, and he was there when you experienced the worst loss you've ever known. He knows; he was with you. And he invites you to record those days and medtiate on how he has used them to prepare you for the calling he has for you. Imagine if you could see a "highlight reel" of your life to help you make sense of your calling.

The highlight reel is a short recap of the best plays from all of sports from the previous week. These videos cut away hundreds of hours of regular play and allow you to focus on a few key moments over a short period of time. There are hundreds of these videos available online, and they are fun to watch. Our goal, as we work through this final portion of the GPS assessment, is to help you create a highlight reel of your spiritual development. This will include your gifts, your passions, and now your story. Bringing these all together will help you see the whole picture.

The questions in the story portion of the assessment are narrative, prompting you to look back over your life and notice where your gifts and passions were being developed at different times. You may find it beneficial to invite a parent, a sibling, or a friend to help you answer the questions from your earlier years. Close friends and spouses can help answer questions from later years.

We encourage you to give this exercise a bit more time. It will require some reflection and thought, but the extra effort you invest in slowing down and listening to Jesus as he brings memories to mind will serve you well. I have received many stories of unexpected inspiration that came from filling out this portion of the assessment, and I trust you will be inspired as well.

To help you prepare, we will share the questions from the assessment, as well as some sample answers. But first we offer a word of caution. People commonly face three challenges in developing their personal highlight reel. Check to see if one of them poses a threat to you. If so, ask a friend to pray for you to push through it. You will be glad you did.

The three challenges are:

1. The false wall between the sacred and secular
2. Guilt and shame from previous indiscretions
3. False humility

Let's take a look at each of these before we wrap up.

The False Wall between the Sacred and Secular

One of the most common challenges to creating your spiritual development highlight reel is the perception that there is a wall between our sacred time and our secular time. We define sacred time as the time we spend at church or doing church-related activities. Secular time is the time we spend doing everything else: participating in sports, pursuing hobbies, working at our job, going to school, doing volunteer work. If we believe that this artificial wall exists, we exclude the valuable spiritual development exercises that we consider secular from our highlight reels. Doing this prevents us from recognizing God's work in the fullness of our lives.

I (Brian) was a huge KISS fan when I was young. Like many elementary school kids of the time, I was starstruck by the theatrical aspect of that band. If you are familiar with KISS, you know there is very little that is sacred about them or their lyrics. That said, KISS influenced me to be comfortable, creative, and alive onstage. Starting in fourth or fifth grade, my friends and I would create KISS concerts in my basement and invite our friends and family to come watch. The record player would play the music (we played tennis rackets), but we created the lights, the outfits, the makeup, and the rest of the show, including a fully functioning TCR racetrack that had the cars looping the track during "Detroit Rock City"!

I do not recall thinking about God during those concerts. They certainly were not church-sponsored events. Those concerts were, however, formative in my life. Watching KISS perform, and then taking their creativity and reproducing it with my friends, was preparation for me to feel alive onstage while teaching hundreds and even thousands of people. KISS influenced me to be meaningfully involved in the creative aspects of developing message series and worship services at our church. If God can use a band like KISS to prepare an elementary school kid for a future role in ministry, he can use anything to prepare you for the work of service he has in mind!

I encourage you to read this next part out loud: "Everything is spiritual. All of life is designed to be sacred. God is redeeming it all." Start tearing down that false wall by allowing yourself to look beyond your church experiences to see how your gifts and passions have been developing in your day-to-day life.

Guilt and Shame from Previous Indiscretions

All of God's children have some regrets. That's pretty normal. But sometimes those regrets can be so intense that we want to forget anything and everything associated with them. Sadly, some of the most significant gifts and passions get sucked into the "regret disposal" of our memories.

Years ago, I (Brian) had a friend who had been a popular radio personality. She was a gifted voice animator, but she didn't want to use that ability, because it reminded her of a time in her life when she made some really poor decisions. It would have been very easy for her to keep her ability buried. We too may be tempted to bury our abilities because of past mistakes or even outright sin. But think about it this way: if there are certain things you have accomplished on your own without Jesus, imagine what you could do *with* Jesus.

That's what happened with my friend. Once she invited Jesus into her past, she was able to resolve her present and use her ability to do great things in our church's ministries. You see, we don't need to allow our past failures to limit our current capacity to love and serve others.

False Humility

False humility is choosing to deny that you have any real gifts, in an effort to appear humble to others (or even to yourself). This is sometimes difficult, because it can look and sound like genuine humility. At the core of false humility, however, is pride. C. S. Lewis described it well: "Humility is not thinking less of yourself. . . . It is thinking of yourself less." Don't downplay what God has made or the gifts he has given. The gifts are there. They have been deposited into you. You did not put them there; God did! To deny their presence is poor stewardship of the things God has entrusted to you. Don't allow self-focused pride to steal opportunities from you!

GATHERING INFORMATION FOR YOUR HIGHLIGHT REEL

Many find it difficult to make a highlight reel, so we have created a series of prompts with sample responses to help in the recollection process. To meaningfully work through these cues, you need to have your results from the gifts and passions portions of the survey.

Read through these questions and sample answers and jot down any memories, big or small, that come to mind. We have received numerous comments on how meaningful this process is, so we wholeheartedly encourage you to create some emotional and spiritual space and let God prompt you to recall the memories he wants included in your highlight reel.

1. *Review your spiritual gifts.* List any memories you have of those gifts being developed or used in your past.

- Example: "My first memory of using my teaching gift was when I was in fourth grade. The neighborhood kids regularly came to my house, and I often played the teacher in our make-believe school."
- Example: "I didn't know it at the time, but I had a leadership gift in high school. I was the class president for four years and led the school to make multiple changes that are still in place today."

2. *Review your natural abilities.* List any memories you have of those abilities being developed or used in your past.

   - Example: "My event planning ability really blossomed in early adulthood, when my best friends started getting married. I offered to plan a girlfriend's wedding, and it went so well that I ended up planning several weddings and baby showers."

3. *Review the people and the causes you selected in the passions section.* Please share any life experiences you have had that potentially developed these passions in you. As a reminder, our greatest passions often emerge out of our greatest struggles.

   - Example: "My passion for helping young marrieds create strong financial plans developed in my middle-age years. I was laid off from my job during the recession and did not have enough money to keep our house. I don't want that to happen to anyone else."

4. *Review your influencing styles.* List any memories you have of those styles being developed or used in your past.

- Example: "I didn't notice I had the apostolic influencing style until I was retired. Throughout my life, I always helped new churches as they were getting started. When I retired, I was asked to be on the board of a church-planting organization because of my 'obvious vision' for seeing more churches planted across the country."

We hope you noticed how these answers are drawn from various life stages. It is our hope that you can pull answers similar to these from all of your life stages. The more highlights you have, the clearer your picture will be!

MOVING FORWARD

When you work through the story portion of the online assessment, you'll be one step closer to creating your highlight reel. And here is the good news: with a highlight reel in place, you now have three fully triangulated signals! You know your top gifts. You understand those gifts and how they are used in God's kingdom. That signal is strong. You know the people and the causes you are most passionate about, and you know your influencing style and how it serves the people of God. That signal is strong. You have a highlight reel that can serve as a record of how God has been developing those gifts and passions throughout your story. That signal is strong.

The next step is to look over your highlight reel and determine where your GPS signals are leading you. There are several questions we ask when watching someone's highlight reel.

What themes are repeated most often? Do you see a thread weaving its way through your story? Does a people group or cause show up again and again? Is there a way that you repeatedly bring a particular value to an organization? If so, that thread probably holds an important clue as to your next step. Write down any repeated themes you notice.

Which memories sparked the most emotion? It is not uncommon for someone to write down a memory that had no relation to the results captured in the gifts and passions portions of the assessment. Often, these memories were prompted by something a parent, sibling, or friend shared with them. If the memory sparked a strong emotion, especially a warm emotion you would feel when connecting with a friend you have not seen in years, then you probably have found an important clue for determining your next step. Even if the emotion was anger, frustration, or sadness, it is possible that those emotions were there because the value of those memories has not been revisited for some time. If it was meaningful in the past, it will probably be meaningful again in the future.

How can your story continue to be written in your church?
If your passion is serving children or youth, most churches
would love for you to begin serving right away! Honestly, this
is true for many of the gifts. People with hospitality gifts are
great at welcoming guests to the church. People with mercy
and encouragement gifts are great prayer partners and counselors. People with shepherding and teaching gifts make
great small group leaders. The list goes on and on. If your
church has a volunteer coordinator, ask them about the best
option for you. If not, ask a pastor or staff person about serving in an area of ministry that fits your gifts and passions.

*How can your story continue to be written in your commu-
nity?* You can use your gifts to serve your neighbors. Most gifts
can be used to serve in your homeowners association, your
neighborhood watch group, or some other civic organization.
You can google the name of your town and look for relocation
services. Many ways to get involved are listed there.

You can use your gifts to serve your small group. All
gifts can be used there. You can teach, you can administrate
serve projects or group outings, you can use your mercy gift
to keep prayer logs and comfort those who are hurting. Small
groups are one of the best gift incubators on the planet!

You can use your gifts to serve a local ministry. There
are 1.5 million not-for-profit organizations in the United
States, and many of them are ministries carrying out the
mission of Jesus in a local area. One of the things I (Brian)
am most proud of in the church I serve is the networking

relationships we have with so many of these ministries in Kansas City. We work with an organization that is reducing teen homelessness. We work with an organization that is mitigating the impact of sex trafficking. We work with an organization that promotes education among the more challenged teens in our urban core.

Every one of these ministries is an opportunity for each of us to take a next step in developing our calling! Want to see a list of organizations in your area? Simply google the words "IRS exempt organizations" and add pertinent information to get a listing. Choose an organization, contact them, and ask about ways to serve.

You can even use your gifts to start your own nonprofit ministry. If you have the appropriate gift mix or a helpful team around you, you can set out to meet a need that is specific to your calling.[13] Is God asking you to start a 501(c)(3)? There are some very helpful organizations and resources that can help you get started.[14]

MAKE THE MOST OF YOUR GPS!

You may have noticed that when we speak of finding your place and living out your calling, we have been using the term ministry. This may be confusing to some people, especially if you tend to think of ministry as something that happens exclusively in a church building on Sunday mornings. Over the years, we've noticed that many people live with an impoverished and unbiblical understanding of ministry. We'd like to change that.

The Greek word that in the New Testament is most often translated as "ministry" is *diakonia*. The fundamental meaning of the word is service. Although most tend to associate the word ministry with ministers—a select few professional clergy—the exact opposite is the case in the New Testament. Ephesians 4:12 is crystal clear that job one for church leaders is to "equip the saints for the work of ministry *[diakonia]*" (NRSV). The ministers don't do all the ministry; they equip so that everyone can do ministry.

What is the origin of this common misunderstanding?

Subconsciously, many followers of Christ still tend to think of life in boxes. We have boxes for our work, our family, our recreation, our social life, our private life, our financial life, and every other area. Everything is compartmentalized. We place most of our lives in secular boxes, areas that are mostly untouched by God. Or at the very least, we assume they aren't all that important to him. When we decide to follow Jesus, we add some sacred boxes to our lives—a church life, a devotional life, a ministry life.

We may think of the devotional box as sacred, but the work box tends to remain devoid of religion. As a pastor, I (Rob) have often heard well-meaning people tell me, "I love being here for the weekend services. I love serving in this volunteer ministry. I can't wait to get here. But when I leave here, it's so draining. Pastor, my work isn't like your work. I spend all day making widgets in a factory. I spend all day making sales calls. I spend all day crunching numbers. I spend my day [fill in the blank]. What I do doesn't matter for eternity."

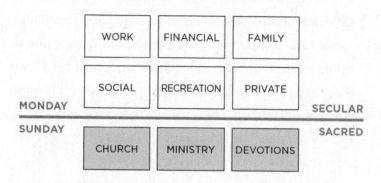

Many people in our churches admit to a deep Sunday-Monday disconnect. And underneath it all is a faulty worldview, one that divides the sacred and the secular. So when many speak of ministry, they are thinking about something religious or something exclusive to Sunday morning.

But is this kind of thinking biblical? No. The Bible takes a battle-ax to this dualistic mindset. The apostle Paul reminds us, "Whether you eat or drink or whatever you do, do it all for the glory of God" (1 Cor. 10:31). He also writes, "Whatever you do, whether in word or deed, do it all in the name of the Lord Jesus, giving thanks to God the Father through him" (Col. 3:17). To drive it home, Paul says, "Whatever you do, work at it with all your heart, as working for the Lord, not for human masters, since you know that you will receive an inheritance from the Lord as a reward. It is the Lord Christ you are serving" (vv. 23–24).

It's clear that the goal of our ministry, as followers of Jesus, is to serve him in everything we do.

In these verses, Paul is proclaiming that everything we do is connected to our ministry. All of life is sacred and filled with a clear purpose—the glory of God. In the cultural mandate and in the church mandate, the goal is the same: we are to do everything for God's glory. The object is to offer the entirety of our world back to God, every nook and cranny. God wants us to eat, play, create, work, celebrate, rest, and relate to one another for his glory.

None of us just "get" this definition of ministry over-night. So we've broken down the various understandings of ministry into three levels that people often progress through in their journey. To begin, let's identify which level of under-standing you are at. Then we want to challenge you to con-sider changing that. Here is a brief summary of each.

Level 1: Ministry = Clergy Only

On this level, Shawn, a heating and cooling system re-pairman, thinks, "I'm a technician. That's secular work. My pastor, he's a minister, and he does the work of ministry. That's something sacred and special to God." Unfortunately, this is an all-too-common understanding of ministry. But it's radically reductive and unbiblical. It imports a division the Bible does not teach into our understanding of ministry, dividing church or religious activities from other aspects of life. In this understanding of ministry, certain trained individuals—the clergy—are the ones responsible for the work of ministry, while the rest of us receive that ministry.

Level 2: Ministry = Volunteerism

At this level, Shawn says, "I'm a technician by day, but I love praying with people. So I'm a volunteer in the prayer ministry of my church. As 'next-step counselors,' members of the prayer team are positioned near the stage after weekend services, ready to pray with people as they respond to what they've experienced. I love it. I'm a technician, but my volunteer ministry role is in the prayer team of my church."

This is probably the most common way people think about ministry. Is it incorrect? Not entirely. Yet as with a level 1 understanding of ministry, it is incomplete. Discovering the power and fulfillment of gift-based ministry in a volunteer role is an important step for many people. But if we think that volunteering in a church program is the endgame, we've missed out on what God wants for us.

Settling for volunteerism would be like saying, "I hope all the soldiers we train in boot camp never leave" or "I hope college students stay on campus to take classes forever." Some of you may have a twentysomething who is on the eight-year college plan, and you can relate!

Many well-meaning Christians and churches settle in at level 2. But the apostle Peter declares, "[We] are a chosen people, a royal priesthood, a holy nation" (1 Peter 2:9). This means that every Christian is called to be a priest who serves God. The Reformation brought back the biblical teaching of the priesthood of all believers, but sadly, many of those insights were never fully applied in the life of the church. That's one of the reasons why we've written this book! We want to unleash every follower of Jesus into ministry, enabling and equipping them to follow their God-given calling in life, way beyond the walls of the church building or the centralized programs of the church.

As followers of Jesus, we are ministers all the time. We are missionaries all the time. It's not something we do; it's who we *are* as the people of God. We need to destroy the caste system that divides our time into sacred and secular and splits the roles of ministry into clergy and laity, professionals and volunteers.

You've been called by Jesus right where you live, work, study, shop, and play. Jesus wants to mobilize his people in every sector of society for ministry all day, everywhere. Why? So his mission is expressed in each sector. You and I, as the church of Jesus, are called to be the light of the world.

Level 3: Ministry = All of Life

We are tempted to call level 3 "The Ordination of All Vocations." In levels 1 and 2, ordination is an event in which a pastor or priest is called apart and commissioned for a life of service to God. We want to extend that to all believers. Your conversion was your commissioning. Your baptism was your ordination. And right now, one of the most exciting things we are hearing is that people are integrating the mission of Jesus into their workplace, their campus, their neighborhood, and the places where they play and shop.

Shawn, the heating and cooling technician, is not just an illustration; he's a real person. And though he's a technician, he's living at level 3. He's doing it through something he calls the "thirty-plus strategy." Shawn adds thirty minutes to every repair or installment appointment, every day, because he's on mission for Jesus. He prays every day that Jesus will give him an opportunity to invest into the people who own the heating and cooling units he's working on. He never forces anything on them. If all they want is business, then he simply uses that extra time to sit in his van and pray for those people. But you'd be shocked by some of the exciting stories Shawn can tell you, in which the door has opened up for further conversation and Shawn ends up praying *with* people instead. While he may be making less money because the thirty-plus strategy means fewer appointments every day, he goes to bed richer each night, knowing he has lived out his calling, both in the quality of his work and in the way he has integrated the mission of Jesus into his work. We think this is a beautiful example of someone integrating a spiritual gift (intercession) into his daily work life where he uses his natural gifts (expertise in HVAC) to add value to the world. You don't need to wait on anything to take a step like this.

Even if your pastor or priest hasn't given you the go-ahead, Jesus has. You have his permission to shift the location and mindset of your ministry. Today, if you want to help fulfill the mission of Jesus, most of your ministry will need to happen *outside* the teams, events, and infrastructure of the organized church.

GO TOGETHER!

In addition to encouraging you to shift the location and mindset of your ministry, we'd like to suggest that you consider doing mission with other people. Jesus sent his disciples out to serve in pairs. Choosing to serve with a friend or a small group of people is more than biblical; it's also fun! Ministry is a team sport, and it's meant to be done together with other followers of Jesus. When you are choosing who to invite with you on this journey, ask yourself these two questions:

1. *"With whom do I have good chemistry?"* Most of our longtime friends are people we have good chemistry with. Ministry can be difficult, and you need your partners to be part of the solution to the challenges you will face.

2. *"Who complements me?"* Another issue in ministry is maintaining balance and utilizing different gifts appropriately. If you are an apostolic influencer, you could benefit from the presence of a shepherding influencer. Ultimately, the best and most effective teams have all five influencing styles at the table, serving together. The real trick is finding people with those different styles whom you trust. You need them to be honest with you, and you need them to disagree with you on occasion for the ministry's benefit.

PREPARING FOR A LONG JOURNEY

Another important consideration as you seek to fulfill your calling is to learn to nurture and develop it. Knowing your calling is a great start, but it needs to be fed and developed. Pastor Rick Warren recommends that to remain current, you should regularly ask yourself two questions: "Am I being fruitful?" and "Am I fulfilled?" Another way to ask the first question is to ask yourself, "Is God still using this ministry to accomplish his purposes?" Is he still doing the life-changing things he was once doing? Is he still advancing his kingdom through your efforts? Another way of asking the second question could be, "Am I still excited about this ministry?"

Do you still look forward to the time you will be engaged in it? Do you still daydream about it?

If you can answer both of these questions with a resounding yes, then you probably are still on track. When you can answer only one of these questions with a resounding yes, it might be time to start looking at other options. Answering one of the questions with a definite no might mean God wants to correct a character issue, or it might be that he is introducing new ministry opportunities into your life. It might be time for a ministry transition, or it could be time to take the GPS assessment again and see if God is refining and renewing your calling.

Remember that Christian calling is fluid and evolving. Being faithful in our current calling often leads to higher responsibility in our calling. And that may call for a change. An excellent way to discern your next step at that point is to retake the GPS assessment. Since it's free, you can take it anytime, as often as you like. Your assessment data will be saved until you choose to delete it.[15]

THE GREATEST STORY EVER TOLD?

The canon of popular literature includes amazing stories like *Gone with the Wind*, *One Flew Over the Cuckoo's Nest*, *War and Peace*, *The Adventures of Huckleberry Finn*, and *The Hobbit*.

The list of great stories goes on and on. Sometimes we find ourselves falling into a trap, as followers of Christ. We make the mistake of trying to write the greatest story ever told with our own life story.

Here is why that's a mistake.

God is the author of your story, and you are called to live out the story he is writing. The problem we face in life comes when we stand in the way of God writing his perfect story through us. Instead we need to ask Jesus to take up the pen and write our lives into the great story that unites all stories—his story.

There are times when we wrestle the pen from Jesus' hand, wanting to take control and define who we are and what our lives should mean. But often during those times, our passion for ministry begins to dwindle away. Thankfully, at just the right moment, Jesus will gently prod us to release the pen back to him so he can start writing again.

Save yourself the pain and frustration. Let Jesus write your story. And here is his amazing promise: if you let him write your story, your life will impact this world in a profound way.

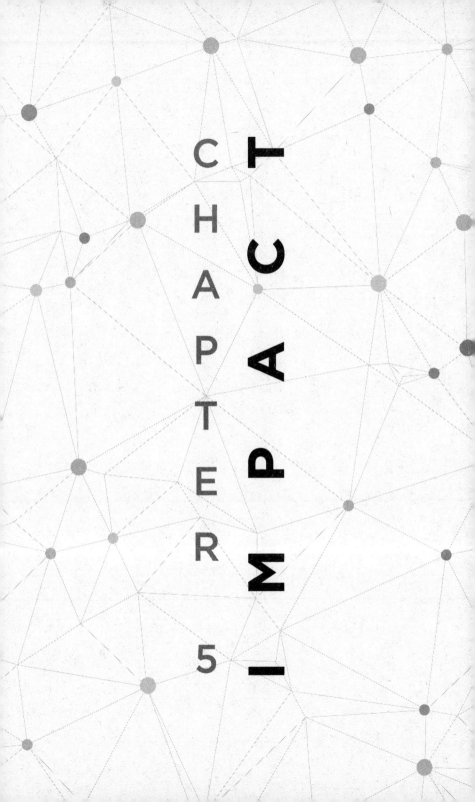

CHAPTER 5

IMPACT

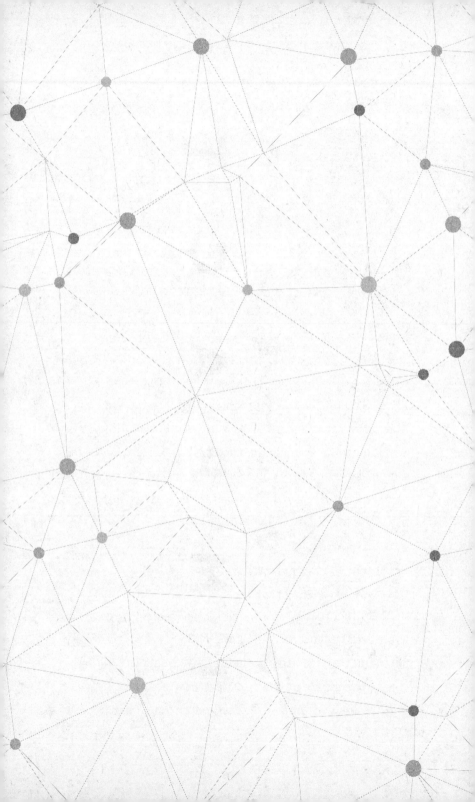

We've talked about the value of GPS technology in helping us find our way, triangulating our position to help us know where we are and how to reach our destination. But GPS is radically changing how we interact with the world around us in other ways as well.

GPS technology has been integrated into tracking chips that allow us to locate almost anything, including pets. Yes, you can have a chip installed right into Fido. Rover, the nation's largest network of pet sitters and walkers, allows pet owners to track their dogs in real time. And because many parents are nervous about letting their kids walk to school, GPS-enabled smartwatches and wristbands for children are also increasing in popularity, allowing parents to follow their kids on an app.

GPS technology can be embedded almost anywhere. Gone are the days of losing keys, phones, wallets, and luggage. You can buy almost anything GPS-enabled, allowing you to track its location. Don't even think about "borrowing" the linens from your hotel. Some companies are now embedding tracking chips into towels and sheets so the hotel will instantly know if a guest has left the property with their goods.[16]

GPS technology is impacting the world of commerce, as brick-and-mortar retailers tap into our phone location and notify us of nearby deals. If you download the Urban Outfitters app, whenever you are close to a store, they will kindly let you know, "The sale's ending! Get in here now!" If you were shopping online for shoes at Macy's earlier this week and decide to visit the shoe section at the physical store today, Macy's will helpfully send you a coupon for those shoes. All of this can make us feel a little uncomfortable, but there is also a trade-off here between being willing to be followed and having access to good bargains. It makes me want to say, "Macy, you're a creeper. Stop the shopper stalking! On second thought, I'll take the coupon. I'm half Dutch after all."

GPS technology is integrated into recreational activities like hiking, running, biking, boating, fishing, and skiing. And GPS is now blurring the line between virtual and actual reality through location-based, augmented reality games like Pokémon Go. The game utilizes the player's mobile GPS to locate, capture, train, and fight virtual creatures called Pokémon, which appear on the screen when players arrive at certain locations. This game has now been downloaded more than five hundred million times.

GPS is changing the world and affecting our lives in ways

that we haven't even begun to recognize. The United States has sixteen critical infrastructure sectors, from energy to agriculture, and all but three of those are now dependent on GPS technology in one way or another.[17] If the GPS satellite system were to crash today, it could be catastrophic. We have grown dependent on GPS technology to keep life in America stable, and that isn't likely to change. GPS technology is one of the key building blocks for emerging technologies that promise even greater impact and efficiency.

We highlight all of this because we see the same—and even greater—potential as you utilize your spiritual GPS by locating your calling through your gifts, passions, and story. We hope this will lead to a massive impact in your life, in your church community, in your neighborhood and workplace, and around the world. As you embrace your calling, GPS can become an integrated way of life, something that affects everything you do. Let's explore the impact potential of GPS in you, through you, and beyond you.

THE IMPACT POTENTIAL OF GPS

As we learned earlier, each one of us is created by God, an incomprehensible work of art. We are fearfully and wonderfully made, and all of our days are written by God before we are born. As believers, we are indwelt by the Holy Spirit, with additional special abilities to carry out God's redemption work. But why were we made with such potential?

God wants to do his powerful work, accomplishing his cosmic purposes in us, through us, and beyond us. We need to respond to his calling by keeping our signals triangulated. Only then can God use our GPS to make an impact. That has certainly been true for Andy.

Andy was involved in a men's disciple-making group that I (Brian) led several years ago. Andy was a faithful churchgoer, but he was not experiencing the full impact of Jesus working in him, through him, and beyond him. Andy had tried to get involved and use his gifts and passions in the church by volunteering to lead the men's ministry. But his initial efforts led to burnout, and he was sidelined for several years. That all changed when he began pursuing his calling through his spiritual GPS.

One of the habits Andy developed in that disciple-making group was daily Bible engagement. Along with the others, Andy would read a selected chapter of the Bible and journal what he learned and what he was going to do with what he learned. Andy was about seven months into the daily practice of this discipline when God spoke to him through his reading of Proverbs 31: "Speak up for those who cannot speak for themselves, for the rights of all who are destitute. Speak up and judge fairly; defend the rights of the poor and needy" (vv. 8–9).

At this point in his life, Andy was the recruitment director for a national company, and the CEO of the company tasked him to develop effective processes that would help that company hire people who had disabilities and maintain meaningful employment relationships with them. Andy had been delaying the project as long as he could. He had no passion for it and no idea how to do it.

Early one morning, before our 5:30 a.m. meeting, Andy was reading the passage in Proverbs 31, and as he was reading, the Spirit of God moved powerfully inside him. He sensed God saying to him, quite clearly, "I want to create those processes through you. I want to bring my power to bear on this project. These people with disabilities are my people, and I am sending you to reach them for me." In an instant, Andy's attitude changed. He now had a people and a cause: giving the disabled a shot at employment and an opportunity to receive dignity through work.

Andy could barely speak when he shared this with our group. He'd never experienced anything like this before. After he shared the experience and his conviction of God's calling, we laid hands on Andy and prayed for him to be able to follow through on his new task. And those prayers were answered. Andy's new passion for the project, and the power of Jesus guiding him to do it, led to a first hire within six months. According to Andy, the implementation of policies and projects of this magnitude are rarely accomplished in twice the time! Within months after that initial hire, Andy was asked to share his developments with other companies, such as Google, and even the White House. His counsel was sought by the National Organization of Disabilities and other organizations. Andy had found his calling.

One year later, Andy left his job and started his own consulting firm. He now serves Starbucks, Hobby Lobby, and other large companies, helping them develop best practices in hiring and maintaining effective working relationships with people who have disabilities. But as powerful as this is, the impact of Andy's life is not limited to his calling. This calling has also led to shifts in his character and his attitude toward people. Andy knows where the power to serve others comes from, and he does not want to lose it. To make sure he stays on track, Andy has created a spiritual accountability board that meets with him every month. In this group, he discloses his challenges, his temptations, and his needs. His friends counsel him and pray for him.

Finding his place in this world has profoundly changed Andy's life. It personifies the words of Colossians 1:27, where Paul speaks of the church as "Christ in you, the hope of glory." You see, Jesus is bearing spiritual fruit in Andy's character. Jesus is working through Andy's spiritual gifts to carry out the cultural mandate. Andy is now a new man.

But Jesus is also changing others through Andy. Most obviously, Jesus is changing the lives of those with disabilities who are being hired and enjoying the dignity and community of employment. As of this writing, more than thirty-five hundred people with disabilities have found positions that can be traced to projects Andy directly helped to develop. Nearly ten thousand people have been hired through projects in which Andy had a consulting role. And Andy has trained more than six thousand people in disability awareness and etiquette, to help them better manage individuals with disabilities.

The numbers are staggering. But even more potent than the numbers are the personal stories that these numbers represent. Here are Andy's words about Kyle, his very first hire.

On Kyle's first day, the general manager called me to tell me that Kyle was there and was proudly wearing his dad's watch. Although it was too big for him, Kyle was very proud to wear it and was making sure he was where he needed to be when he needed to be there. That in itself made me feel good inside.

Three weeks later, I received another call from Kyle's general manager, who told me that he had to tell me about Kyle. Frankly, I was fearing the worst. However, the GM asked me if I remembered the call a few weeks earlier about Kyle wearing his father's watch. I emphatically said yes, but the GM said he had an update. Today Kyle came in with a watch that fits him and that he bought with his first ever paycheck! That is probably one of the first times I shed a tear on a business call.

But the story of Kyle doesn't stop there. He was the first associate to score a perfect score on an observed assessment by his managers, not just at his location and not just in Kansas City but in the Midwest region of our company that stretches from Minnesota to Texas and from Colorado to Illinois.

Kyle continues to work. Kyle has moved out of his parents' home and into a residential facility, where he has roommates. This is what he has always wanted! Kyle has insurance and still makes people smile at work. But even further, Kyle's parents have said they no longer feel that they have to live one day longer than Kyle to be sure he is taken care of. They know he will be fine.

As a member of Andy's accountability team, I know how dedicated he is to loving his family and involving them in mission with him. He regularly involves his wife and children in helping him make business decisions that will impact his time. This sense of common mission has made an impact on his entire family, including his son Gabe.

When Gabe was in third grade, we received a phone call from his teacher. Needless to say, she had our attention! She stated she was calling to tell us about an incident that occurred on the playground earlier in the week. There was a boy in another class, in the same grade as Gabe, who has special needs. During lunch, the classes would participate in 'walk-n-talk,' which was basically kids walking around the track during a portion of their lunchtime. She said that Gabe went over to him and just started talking to him and walked with him all around the track. This was not an isolated event, however. Gabe didn't only do it on one day but had done it all five days of that week!

Gabe always has been very social and was also a member of the football team. As the week progressed, members of the team would come walk with Gabe, and he was introducing him to the other boys as they came over. In short, the boy from the other class went from walking by himself to now having a group of guys walking with him every day.

I was surprised that Gabe had not told us about this really cool thing he was doing. I was curious as to why he did not tell me, so I asked him about it after the teacher's phone call. Gabe said, "Dad, it was just not a big deal. It is what *we* do. We speak up for those who can't speak up for themselves."

Jesus has made an impact in Andy's life. And Jesus is making an impact through Andy and beyond Andy. A famous saying tells us that "you can count the apples on the tree, but who can count the apples in a seed?" It's easy to see the immediate impact Jesus has in you. And we can see some of the impact Jesus has through us. But it's far more difficult to grasp the impact Jesus has beyond us. We may never fully know how we were used by God in this life. But that should never be a reason to not pray and ask for that work to happen.

The impact you and I will have on this planet, at this time in history, is more than the sum of our individual contributions. I recall standing in Jerusalem's Church of the Holy Sepulcher, looking at the mosaic of Jesus being nailed to the cross. It is remarkable how that single image was made up of thousands of very small monochromatic tiles. Like the individual tiles in that mosaic, our lives play only one small part of Jesus' restoration plan. Like a master artist, Jesus is taking our callings and crafting them together to paint a powerful and compelling redemption story for the world to see and respond to. Because of this, it is incredibly important for us to play our part, regardless of how insignificant it may seem to us. The story of Edward Kimball illustrates this powerfully.

There is a good chance you have never heard of Edward Kimball. Edward was a Sunday school teacher who took his calling seriously. He wanted each of his students to know what it means to have a saving relationship with Jesus. One of the young men in his class was Dwight L. Moody, who grew up to become a famous evangelist and church leader. God used Moody to reach and inspire thousands of people with the love of Jesus. One of those inspired by Moody was a man named Wilbur Chapman, who also became an effective evangelist for Jesus. A professional ballplayer named Billy Sunday attended one of Chapman's evangelistic rallies and was moved to become part of Chapman's team. Before long, Sunday himself was leading his own evangelistic crusades.

One of Billy Sunday's crusades was in Charlotte, North Carolina. The rally was so effective, a group of business leaders was formed to maintain the evangelistic fervor in that area. That group invited another evangelist, Mordecai Ham, to come and preach in Charlotte ten years later. And it was during those evangelistic sessions that Billy Graham became a follower of Jesus. Most people recognize the name of Billy Graham. Graham provided spiritual counsel to every president from Harry Truman to Barack Obama, and he preached to more than 215 million people in more than 180 countries. Graham reached hundreds of millions more through his televised events and radio shows.

It's difficult to imagine another individual who has had more spiritual impact than Billy Graham. But Graham's impact is not an isolated event. What we want you to see is that Billy Graham would have never had the impact he had without Edward Kimball playing his part, faithfully teaching his Sunday school class. Edward Kimball was a seed, and God did a great work in, through, and beyond him.

You are a seed. Will you allow God to do his work in, through, and beyond you?

THE NEXT STEP: DISCIPLE MAKING

As we close, we have one last question for you to consider.

Knowing your GPS is a first step. Our hope is that in reading this book and taking the online assessment, you've begun to recognize the gifts God has given you. Maybe you've started to sense the passions you have for serving others. And perhaps you're able to align your story with the story of Jesus.

There is one last thing we want you to know. Jesus has a common destination imbedded in every GPS—a purpose that fits each of us who are called to follow him. It's a mission he has given to all of us, something that includes our callings and keeps us on the path of following him in mission and expanding his work into the lives of others.

Jesus wants us to multiply. "Then Jesus came to them and said, 'All authority in heaven and on earth has been given to me. Therefore go and make disciples of all nations, baptizing them in the name of the Father and of the Son and of the Holy Spirit, and teaching them to obey everything I have commanded you. And surely I am with you always, to the very end of the age'" (Matt. 28:18–20).

This can be summarized in one phrase: disciple making. Disciples are learners or apprentices who live in full surrender to Jesus as their master and teacher. When people become disciples of Jesus, they are transformed in their character and calling. As they grow in character and calling, their impact increases. They are mobilized to make a difference in every sector of society and every nook and cranny of the world. The genius of Jesus is that he is able to perfectly design billions of different GPS's and deploy them at the right place, at the right time, in order to fully manifest his kingdom.

When Jesus told us to pray, "Let your kingdom come, let your will be done on earth as it is in heaven" (Matt. 6:10 GWT), he was teaching us to pray for a revolution. It's about joining Jesus in bringing "up there" down here, bringing the life of heaven into life here on earth. It is what the Old Testament prophets called *shalom*. It is not just "peace" as some vague sense of well-being but rather the total restoration of wholeness in every area of a person's life and every area of the world.

Cornelius Plantinga, president of Calvin Theological Seminary, in his book *Not the Way It's Supposed to Be*, describes this idea as follows: "The webbing together of God, humans, and all creation in justice, fulfillment, and delight is what the Hebrew prophets call shalom. We call it peace, but it means far more than mere peace of mind or a cease-fire between enemies. In the Bible, shalom means universal flourishing, wholeness, and delight—a rich state of affairs in which natural needs are satisfied and natural gifts fruitfully employed, a state of affairs that inspires joyful wonder as its Creator and Savior opens doors and welcomes the creatures in whom he delights. Shalom, in other words, is the way things ought to be."[18]

Jesus came to proclaim that the kingdom of God was at hand. And in so doing, he was giving a vision of the future. Jesus proclaimed his life, death, and resurrection as the only pathway for us to move from being a part of the problem—sick with sin unto death—to part of the solution: disciples filled with life eternal. Jesus said that he came that we might have life and have it to the full!

And Jesus had one master plan for all of this to happen: making disciples.

Through disciple making, Jesus creates the change in us that needs to be manifested in the world. As we become disciples who make disciples, we fill the earth, spreading throughout the planet like yeast in dough (Matt. 13:33). Without personal transformation and the multiplication of disciples, world transformation cannot be achieved or sustained. You can think of disciple making as the operating system that all the GPS satellites run on, coordinating all of our individual callings and positions into one master purpose, one master plan—the kingdom of God.

Years ago, I (Rob) almost train-wrecked my marriage pursuing my GPS at the expense of my family. I had lost sight of God's kingdom purposes as the ultimate goal of my life. I lost sight of the main thing, that I was called to be a disciple of Jesus, with my identity rooted in Christ, resting in the gospel as my means and motive. And I'd forgotten that my primary calling was ultimately to make disciples and that starts at home.

As wonderful as it is to know our GPS, our calling in life, we need to align our GPS to the right satellite and make sure we are working for the purposes of God's kingdom, making disciples of Jesus who make disciples. Todd Wilson describes this masterfully in his book *Multipliers: Leading beyond Addition*: "We need to mobilize followers of Jesus on their secondary calling. But we should always keep the perspective that he gives us our secondary callings [GPS] to fulfill our primary calling. If I focus on growing the fullness of Jesus in me and seek to carry that fullness to others as I make disciples, my secondary callings will uniquely position me for engaging those in my unique mission field. I have to learn to properly contextualize my unique calling and burden with his core cause and purpose."[19]

The famous Puritan preacher Cotton Mather described it this way: We are in a rowboat and there are two oars. One oar is our primary calling—to be a disciple who makes disciples. The other oar is our personal calling—living out the gifts, passions, and story God has given to us. Some people never put either oar in the water, and they float aimlessly through life. Others put only one oar in the water, and they end up going in circles. To move ahead, we must learn to pull on both oars.

As we pull both oars, we unite our personal calling to the broader mission of Jesus and begin making disciples who make disciples who plant churches that plant churches. Through this, movements of personal transformation become the sustaining force for world transformation. We are all called to be disciples who makes disciples. Jesus made that much clear. And as those disciples and churches multiply, they fill a neighborhood, a city, a nation, and the world. And as this movement spreads, Jesus, in his infinite genius, has distributed the perfect GPS directions into the right individuals at the right places at the right time. He provides the direction we need to identify and slay the Goliaths which keep his kingdom from being fully expressed in our neighborhood, city, nation, and world.[20]

You can see that this invitation will require all of you. You'll be journeying without the old-school map that charts the ordinary, expected, sane, and tame. Instead you'll be following Jesus Christ, Son of the living God, who is calling to you, "Follow me." He has given you the GPS you need to find your way in *the* Way.

Let the journey begin!

CONCLUSION

We started this journey with Map-man, someone who had forgone the advantages of GPS, preferring to rely on crumpled paper and his best guess. It almost cost him his life, and my wife's as well!

Not good.

You've now been given access to your soul GPS—gifts, passions, and story—designed to help you find your place, your calling. The question you must ask yourself is, "Will I tune in those signals and let the Spirit of God lead me in the direction of the one-of-a-kind, masterpiece mission I was made for?"

Map-man was probably wrestling with the map because that was what he was comfortable with, thinking, "Who wants to mess around with that newfangled technology, especially if you're in a hurry?"

Like most people, you've got a lot going on. You'll be tempted to just keep driving. Or to settle for whatever directions you can figure out on your own. But if you do, you'll

185

miss the road Jesus has *for you* that will take you to your personal calling. If you miss that road, you'll miss the purpose you were created for. You'll never find your place.

That would be a tragedy.

On the other hand, GPS could get you to exactly where you are meant to be. You can find your place in this world!

"Open the app," engage this GPS process, get some companions for the journey, and get moving. You'll miss some turns along the way, but that's no problem, as long as you let the Spirit of God redirect you. If you listen, "your ears will hear a voice behind you, saying, 'This is the way; walk in it'" (Isa. 30:21).

I (Rob) listened, and Jesus redirected me to Kansas City, where I've found a place and partners to live out my calling like never before. This book is the byproduct of that! I've found my place.

Jamie, our friend who led the men's fireside group, heard the "voice-by-voice" directions coming through his GPS. Those directions moved him from sales to a key role as an advocate and executive leader of a nonprofit that is changing the future of some of the most marginalized people in his town. Jamie has found his place.

Andy listened to the GPS signals, and the project he had shoved to the back of his desk became the on-ramp to his calling to empower the disabled. Andy has found his place.

I (Brian) recently made one of the most significant career changes in my life because of my GPS signals. After I had been an ordained pastor in a local church for twenty-two years, Jesus guided me to step out of that role and start Disciples Made, a 501(c)(3) ministry that is focused on helping people develop their calling and Christlike character. I get to help hundreds of churches leverage this spiritual GPS to unleash the callings of thousands of people. I have found my place!

We could tell you stories all day long. Like my friend Angie, who went from being a fearful new small groups director to being a disciple-making movement leader in her church. Or my friend Phil, whom Jesus led to leave his increasingly lucrative career in banking to provide spiritual leadership to students growing up on our military bases. I could even mention Karol, who was once afraid to attend church because of her past choices but who has now founded her own 501(c)(3) ministry to help others face the same issues she did earlier in life. My friend Anthony is no longer a ministry consumer. He is now living life fully alive as he builds his own disciple-making movement with men.

But enough of our stories. Now it's your turn. Your gifts, passions, and story can and will locate your calling. Find your place.

NOTES

1. Rick Warren, *The Purpose Driven Church* (Grand Rapids: Zondervan, 1995).
2. H. W. Hoehner, "Ephesians," in J. F. Walvoord and R. B. Zuck, eds., *The Bible Knowledge Commentary: An Exposition of the Scriptures*, vol. 2 (Wheaton, IL: Victor, 1985), 624.
3. *http://fortune.com/2017/09/01/ job-satisfaction-highest-since-2005/.*
4. *www.wsj.com/articles/americans-are-happier-at-work-but-expect -a-lot-less-1504258201.*
5. *www.psychologytoday.com/blog/reading-between-the-headlines/ 201305/white-middle-age-suicide-in-america-skyrockets.*
6. Ibid.
7. Jonathan Jones, "Virginia Ends Historic Season by Suffering Biggest Upset in College Basketball History," *Sports Illustrated* (March 17, 2018), *https://www.si.com/college-basketball/2018/03/ 17/umbc-upsets-virginia-16-beats-1-seed.*
8. Nancy Pearcey, *Total Truth* (Wheaton, IL: Crossway, 2005), 47.
9. Alan Hirsch is the leading author and working theologian on the restoration of the fivefold giftings in Ephesians 4, as well as a mentor and spiritual father to me (Rob). This section is the synthesis and overflow of many conversations and the following books: *The Forgotten Ways: Reactivating Apostolic Movements, The Permanent Revolution: Apostolic Imagination*

and Practice in the 21st Century, and *5Q: Reactivating the Original Intelligence and Capacity of the Body of Christ*.

10. Mike Breen and Steve Cockram, *Building a Discipling Culture*, 2nd ed. (Pawleys Island: 3DMinistries, 2011), 150–53.

11. Alan Hirsch and Tim Catchim, *The Permanent Revolution Playbook: APEST for the People of God: A Six Week Exploration*, Kindle ed. (Denver: Missio, 2014), Kindle locations 1241–46.

12. Erik Reese, *S.H.A.P.E.: Finding and Fulfilling Your Unique Purpose for Life* (Grand Rapids: Zondervan, 2008), 97.

13. I just went through that process myself. Disciples Made is an organization I created to provide churches with turnkey disciple-making processes and experiences. I was inspired to do this by others in our church who had done the same. Kids are getting unexpected birthday gifts because someone started a ministry. Kids are getting meals on the weekend and during the summer when school is out because someone started a ministry.

14. I personally used StartCHURCH because they are faith based and I had heard so many good things about them. They were very helpful and successful in helping me get started well. You can also contact an attorney or other online agencies such as LegalZoom.

15. The very best way to optimize your calling is in a small group that is focused on developing both calling and character. Disciples Made, the disciple-making process we created, is a turnkey solution for that. Followers Made, the first phase of the Disciples Made process, is a six-month journey that helps you talk through and develop your GPS results with up to twelve others. Leaders Made, the second phase of the Disciples Made process, is a ten-month journey that empowers people to optimize their calling for maximum kingdom impact. You can experience both Followers Made and Leaders Made with as few as two other people. Simply go to *www.disciplesmade. com* and get your group started today.

16. "8 Ways to Track Just About Anything with GPS," *www.rd.com/advice/travel/gps-tracking/*.

17. "GPS Is Everywhere, Is That a Good Thing?" *www.wbur.org/hereandnow/2016/05/10/gps-is-everywhere*.

18. Cornelius Plantinga Jr., *Not the Way It's Supposed to Be: A Breviary of Sin* (Grand Rapids: Eerdmans, 1995).

19. Todd Wilson, *Multipliers: Leading beyond Addition* (Arlington, VA: Exponential Resources, 2017).

20. We have created a suite of disciple-making experiences that will equip you to be a disciple who can make disciples who plant churches that plant churches:

- Followers Made: a six-month experience to help you discover your character and calling, equipping you to be a disciple and make disciples.
- Leaders Made: a twelve-month experience to help you discover servant leadership and what it means to lead a community on mission.
- BLESS Learning Community: a six-month experience to help you develop a lifestyle around five incarnational rhythms that equip you to be a missionary where you live, work, study, shop, and play.
- Simple Church Learning Community: a twelve-month experience that equips you step-by-step in planting a simple form of church—an extended spiritual family living on mission together—where you live, work, study, or play.

You can visit *www.disciplesmade.com* or download the Disciples Made app to learn more. In essence, these are the OS that your GPS can run on. Run GPS as an OS, and it will crash. Run GPS on the OS of disciple making, and it leads to the life you've always wanted.